THE COMPLETE BOOK OF FORMS FOR MANAGING THE EARLY CHILDHOOD PROGRAM

THE COMPLETE BOOK OF FORMS FOR MANAGING THE EARLY CHILDHOOD PROGRAM

Kathleen Pullan Watkins, Ed.D.

Lucius Durant, Jr., M.Ed.

THE CENTER FOR APPLIED RESEARCH IN EDUCATION
West Nyack, New York 10995

10 9 8 7 6 5 4 3 2 1

Library of Congress Cataloging-in-Publication Data

Watkins, Kathleen Pullan.
The complete book of forms for managing the early childhood program / Kathleen Pullan Watkins, Lucius Durant.
p. cm.
Includes bibliographical references.
ISBN 0-87628-232-X
1. Nursery schools--Administration. 2. Day care centers--Administration. 3. Education, Preschool--Forms. I. Durant, Lucius, (date) . II. Center for Applied Research in Education.
III. Title.
LB2822.7.W38 1990
372.21--dc20 89-77156
CIP

ISBN 0-87628-232-X

THE CENTER FOR APPLIED RESEARCH IN EDUCATION
BUSINESS & PROFESSIONAL DIVISION
A division of Simon & Schuster
West Nyack, New York 10995

Printed in the United States of America

In joyful and loving remembrance of
Rev. Francis Joseph Dinkel,
Barbara Dinkel Pullan,
Anna Mae Brown,
and
Bennie C. Durant

CONTENTS

ABOUT THIS BOOK

The purpose of *The Complete Book of Forms for Managing the Early Childhood Program* is to give day care providers and preschool staff tools for planning, implementing, and evaluating sound and appropriate programs for young children. It was written largely in response to current trends, which have led in some cases to deterioration of the quality of child care and licensed facilities.

In growing numbers, a broad range of Americans today are entering the preschool and day care fields. Reasons include the much-publicized need for day care services, perceptions of day care as an "easy-to-operate" business, and the possibility of a low-cost initial investment. Furthermore, parents are eager for programs that will provide their preschoolers with a head start. While many in the early childhood and child care professions deplore these developments and are lobbying for increased regulation of programs and training of personnel, the social and legislative changes necessary to assure the highest quality preschool programs cannot be realized in the short-term. There is a need for the kind of immediate help provided in this book.

This book of forms gives preschool and day care educators a one-stop source for effective management tools covering all aspects of their work. For quick access and easy use, the forms are grouped into eight distinct sections corresponding to different functions of the early childhood facility and printed in a big 8½" x 11" spiral-bound format that folds flat for photocopying. All are ready to be reproduced as they appear or to be easily tailored to fit the specific needs of your own program.

Each of the eight sections of the book focuses on one component of the average program. An introduction identifying issues and providing direction for the use of the forms begins each section. The forms are of several different kinds. Some are purely informational, such as Form 5–4, which presents guidelines for individualizing programs for children. Others are meant to provide a format for recording data unique to each program; the "Staff Evaluation Form" in Section 4 is an example of this type. Each section concludes with a bibliography of readings to help providers access additional information in topic areas. Every effort has been made to ensure that the readings are informative, up to date, and of practical use.

Here is a brief overview of the topics and forms featured in the eight sections of this book:

- Section 1 is devoted to administrative and managerial aspects of day care and preschool programs. It discusses incorporation and tax-exemption procedures as well as establishment of an administrative structure, a policy board, and bylaws.
- The second section addresses issues of day care licensing and regulation, and preschool accreditation. These topics are broadly dealt with in view of the wide variance in state and local standards across the United States. Forms included and issues discussed relate to site selection, zoning for school and day care facilities, building renovation and maintenance, and licensing procedures.
- Fiscal management is the subject of Section 3. Emphasis is placed on budget preparation, record keeping, and income tax issues for profit-making programs. Fee collection, grant applications, and other forms for fund raising are also covered in this section.
- Section 4 provides a wealth of information related to preschool personnel. Samples of an employment application, interview questionnaire, employment contract, staff medical forms, new employee orientation agenda, staff roles and responsibilities, and staff evaluation forms are included.
- Aspects of planning the program for children are addressed in Section 5. Identifying goals and objectives; developing unit, lesson, and environmental plans; and selecting equipment and materials are the focus of this section.
- Child and family involvement is the subject of Section 6, which is directed toward the preschool or day care program's relationship with clients. Forms related to admissions, child health histories, developmental screening of youngsters, and parental involvement in the program are included.
- Section 7 covers public-relations issues. Recruiting for programs using various advertising measures is explored. Many tools, such as brochures, newsletters, and volunteer worker programs, for networking with the community are discussed with accompanying forms provided.
- The final section, "Resources for Early Childhood Education," contains lists of sources of materials and equipment, groups for networking, curriculum guides, and other information useful to program providers.

We wish to emphasize that this book can be valuable to all persons who provide preschool services. While the first two sections may be most useful to those with administrative roles, other sections are broadly applicable to those in a variety of staff positions in many types of facilities. Classroom teachers, aides, assistants, volunteers, board members, and students preparing to work with preschool children will all find useful information.

Our intention was to include sample forms covering topics and needs broad enough to apply to early childhood programs throughout the country. If there are omissions, it is likely that they are due to the regionalized nature of an issue or topic.

ACKNOWLEDGMENTS

The authors wish to express deepest appreciation to the following persons for their assistance with this project: Jewel Morrisette-N'dulula, Marian Giles, Ernestine Redd, Harold Sadofsky, Evelyn Fazio, and Win Huppuch. To our families, our loving thanks for your support in all our endeavors.

KATHLEEN PULLAN WATKINS, ED.D.

LUCIUS DURANT, JR., M.ED.

ABOUT THE AUTHORS

KATHLEEN PULLAN WATKINS, ED.D., has held a wide range of positions in the field of early childhood education during a twenty-year career working with young children and their parents. She has directed teacher training programs at Community College of Philadelphia and Chestnut Hill College.

In recent years, Dr. Watkins has consulted for numerous early childhood, health, and human-service programs, usually with Lucius Durant, Jr., her coauthor and partner in Durant and Watkins Associates. Their firm specializes in staff training, program development, and evaluation activities with agencies across the country.

Dr. Watkins is currently a professor of child development in the School of Social Administration at Temple University.

LUCIUS DURANT, JR., M.ED., has had a diversified professional life as an early childhood educator and staff trainer for school personnel at all levels. Mr. Durant has served in a full range of teaching and administrative positions in the day care field, becoming involved in teacher education in 1973 as a leader in Child Development Associate training programs. He currently holds adjunct teaching positions at Community College of Philadelphia and Pennsylvania State University.

As a partner in Durant and Watkins Associates, Mr. Durant has consulted for Head Start, day care, primary school, and community service agencies. He originated the "partnership" concept, which is one of the chief tools utilized and demonstrated by the firm when providing consultant services.

Mr. Durant is currently a training instructor for the Office of Human Resources, School District of Philadelphia.

THE COMPLETE BOOK OF FORMS FOR MANAGING THE EARLY CHILDHOOD PROGRAM

section 1

ADMINISTRATION OF PROGRAMS FOR YOUNG CHILDREN

This first section of *The Complete Book of Forms for Managing the Early Childhood Program* begins with three management tools for use in starting a new preschool business: Steps to Incorporation of Programs (Figure 1–1), Obtaining Tax-Exempt Status (Figure 1–2), and Application for Recognition of Exemption (Figure 1–3). A variety of aids for developing an underlying program philosophy and direction make up the remainder of the section.

SETTING THE TONE

While a great many tasks fall to the administrator, the one most important task could be called "tone setting." Whether starting a program from scratch or picking up a job begun long ago by someone else, the director must set a direction of leadership. That direction setting takes several forms. One of these is the demeanor of the administrator. He or she should inspire confidence, be task-oriented, have the ability to prioritize, and know how to tackle and solve problems.

Another of the mechanisms for setting a positive tone is found in the set of written documents developed by the director and the administrative or policy board of the program. These statements provide guidelines by which a program operates. They can never be assumed to be understood, but must be put into writing.

The program's philosophy and policies must be written for several critical reasons. Putting a program's philosophy in writing eliminates guesswork regarding its intent. The theoretical and other underlying themes of the program are clearly stated for the benefit of those who utilize them as well as for those persons who merely want to hear about the program. Figure 1–4, "Criteria for Developing Program Philosophy," identifies considerations that should be taken into account when developing a program philosophy, and Figure 1–5 offers a complete sample program philosophy.

Failure to make policies and procedures clear is one of the single most common causes of administrative problems. Participants (staff or parents) may behave inappropriately not because of any desire to create problems, but because they are unfamiliar with the program's policies. Moreover, many written policies are incomplete. They lack the concise information that permits smooth functioning of the program and the cooperation of everyone involved. Figures 1–6 and 1–7 present useful criteria for developing policies and sample policies.

Failure to create policies can have implications for families served as well as for staff. For example, it is imperative that administrators consider the creation of a policy regarding AIDS victims. If a staff member contracts AIDS can he or she continue working? Under what circumstances? If a child contracts AIDS can he or she continue to attend the program? Under what circumstances?

There are also important legal reasons to have detailed program policies and procedures. A program may be considered negligent if an accident or illness results from the failure to make policies clear.

It is not only early childhood-center based programs that need to be concerned about stating a philosophy, policies, and procedures. Family day care homes face similar problems when parents fail to understand and comply with a provider's requests. Policies and procedures can outline the recourse of the provider and the consequences for the parent when policies are violated.

ADMINISTRATIVE STRUCTURE

In the same way that written philosophy and policies provide guidelines for staff and parents, a chart showing administrative structure and written guidelines for board members clarifies the roles of persons involved in program operations. Figures 1–8, 1–9, and 1–10 present sample administrative structures, guidelines for policy board members, and sample bylaws. Although it is generally the role of the policy board members to develop an administrative structure and bylaws, a program administrator should be asked to participate or provide input.

With the development of a set of foundational materials, a director or family day care provider has the basis for a smooth-running program. While these documents naturally cannot prevent all problems, many can be avoided if the language used is clear and care is taken to cover all key policy areas.

Figure 1–1

STEPS TO INCORPORATION OF PROGRAMS

Step 1: Review the state statutes regarding incorporation in your state. Check your local library or law library for a copy of the *Martindale-Hubbell Law Directory,* which will provide you with a summary of the applicable statutes.

Step 2: Write to the designated agency in your state and request a copy of the forms and information necessary to form a corporation.

Step 3: The same agency will provide information regarding the availability of your corporate name. You may not use the name of an existing program or agency found elsewhere in your state.

Step 4: Develop and file Articles of Incorporation for your agency. The Articles should include the following information:

1. The names and addresses of persons forming the corporation
2. The name of the corporation
3. The designated period for which the corporation will exist; in the case of a preschool or day care center the designation would be "perpetual"
4. The purposes for which the corporation is organized
5. The number of shares of stock to be issued by the corporation, when appropriate
6. Provisions for permitting or denying stockholders the right to purchase additional stock
7. Information regarding the administration and daily operations of the agency
8. Address of the present office of the corporation
9. The number of directors on the initial board, and their names and addresses

Step 5: Pay the filing fee, which is under $100 in most states.

Step 6: Hold a meeting to organize the corporation. During this meeting the incorporators should:

1. Elect the directors of the board, and the officers
2. Adopt a set of bylaws (see Figure 1–10)
3. Adopt a corporate seal
4. Adopt a stock certificate for issuance to stockholders

Please note that a corporate kit containing most of the necessary materials is available at many stationery stores.

Figure 1–2

OBTAINING TAX-EXEMPT STATUS

A program or agency may wish to file for tax-exempt status in order to qualify for certain types of funding. Many federal or foundation grants are available only to tax-exempt agencies. Furthermore, tax-exemption means that some local and federal taxes can be avoided, and businesses are often persuaded to provide goods or services on a discounted basis to tax-exempt corporations.

Tax exemption does not mean that a business cannot make money. However, profits must be put back into the business; for example, for improvements of the physical plant, for salaries, or for new equipment.

Becoming a nonprofit organization is not automatic. An early childhood program must apply for tax exemption under a section of the Code of the Internal Revenue Service. There are forms to fill out and criteria to be met. Some of the agencies that qualify for exemption are

1. Religious, charitable, or educational organizations
2. Civic or community organizations operated exclusively for the promotion of the public good
3. Churches or associations of churches
4. Veterans organizations
5. Foundations or trusts benefiting the public

It is wise to contact the Internal Revenue Service to obtain the proper forms for applying for nonprofit status. In all cases agencies must file the proper forms each year to declare the agency's financial earnings. In many cases taxes must be paid on unrelated business income, which may be the result of activities unrelated to the primary business of the agency; as in the case of a day care center that profits from a second business operated by the agency director. Generally speaking, bake sales, fairs, fashion shows, buffet dinners, and other forms of public entertainment designed to raise money for the nonprofit agency are exempt from taxation.

Figure 1–3

Form **1023** (Rev. March 1986) Department of the Treasury Internal Revenue Service

Application for Recognition of Exemption
Under Section 501(c)(3) of the Internal Revenue Code

For Paperwork Reduction Act Notice, see page 1 of the instructions.

OMB No. 1545-0056
Expires 3-31-89

To be filed in the key district for the area in which the organization has its principal office or place of business.

This application, when properly completed, constitutes the notice required under section 508(a) of the Internal Revenue Code so that an applicant may be treated as described in section 501(c)(3) of the Code, and the notice required under section 508(b) for an organization claiming not to be a private foundation within the meaning of section 509(a). (**Read the instructions for each part carefully before making any entries.**) If required information, a conformed copy of the organizing and operational documents, or financial data are not furnished, the application will not be considered on its merits and the organization will be notified accordingly. Do not file this application if the applicant has no organizing instrument (see Part II).

Part I Identification

1 Full name of organization	2 Employer identification number **(If none, see instructions)**
3a Address (number and street)	Check here if applying under section: ☐ 501(e) ☐ 501(f) ☐ 501(k)
3b City or town, state, and ZIP code	4 Name and telephone number of person to be contacted ( )
5 Month the annual accounting period ends / 6 Date incorporated or formed	7 Activity codes

8 Has the organization filed Federal income tax returns or exempt organization information returns? . . . . . . ☐ Yes ☐ No
If "Yes," state the form number(s), years filed, and Internal Revenue office where filed.

Part II Type of Entity and Organizational Document (see instructions)

Check the applicable entity box below and attach a **conformed** copy of the organization's organizing document and bylaws as indicated for each entity.

☐ Corporation—Articles of incorporation and bylaws. ☐ Trust—Trust indenture. ☐ Other—Constitution or articles of association and bylaws.

Part III Activities and Operational Information

1 What are or will be the organization's sources of financial support? List in order of size.

2 Describe the organization's fund-raising program, both actual and planned, and explain to what extent it has been put into effect. (Include details of fund-raising activities such as selective mailings, formation of fund-raising committees, use of professional fund raisers, etc.) Attach representative copies of solicitations for financial support.

I declare under the penalties of perjury that I am authorized to sign this application on behalf of the above organization and I have examined this application, including the accompanying statements, and to the best of my knowledge it is true, correct, and complete.

(Signature) (Title or authority of signer) (Date)

Part III Activities and Operational Information (Continued)

3 Give a **detailed** narrative description of the organization's past, present, and proposed future activities, and the purposes for which it was formed. The narrative should identify the specific benefits, services, or products the organization has provided or will provide. If the organization is not fully operational, explain what stage of development its activities have reached, what further steps remain for it to become fully operational, and when such further steps will take place. (**Do not state the purposes and activities of the organization in general terms or repeat the language of the organizational documents.**) If the organization is a school, hospital, or medical research organization, include enough information in your description to clearly show that the organization meets the definition of that particular activity that is contained in the instructions for Part VI-A.

4 The membership of the organization's governing body is:

a Names, addresses, and titles of officers, directors, trustees, etc.	b Annual compensation

Part III Activities and Operational Information (Continued)

4 c Do any of the above persons serve as members of the governing body by reason of being public officials or being appointed by public officials? . . . . ☐ Yes ☐ No
If "Yes," name those persons and explain the basis of their selection or appointment.

d Are any members of the organization's governing body "disqualified persons" with respect to the organization (other than by reason of being a member of the governing body) or do any of the members have either a business or family relationship with "disqualified persons?" (See the Specific Instructions for line 4d.) . . . . ☐ Yes ☐ No
If "Yes," explain.

e Have any members of the organization's governing body assigned income or assets to the organization, or is it anticipated that any current or future member of the governing body will assign income or assets to the organization? . . . . ☐ Yes ☐ No
If "Yes," attach a complete explanation stating which applies and including copies of any assignments plus a list of items assigned.

5 Does the organization control or is it controlled by any other organization? . . . . ☐ Yes ☐ No
Is the organization the outgrowth of another organization, or does it have a special relationship to another organization by reason of interlocking directorates or other factors? . . . . ☐ Yes ☐ No
If either of these questions is answered "Yes," explain.

6 Is the organization financially accountable to any other organization? . . . . ☐ Yes ☐ No
If "Yes," explain and identify the other organization. Include details concerning accountability or attach copies of reports if any have been submitted.

7 a What assets does the organization have that are used in the performance of its exempt function? (Do not include property producing investment income.) If any assets are not fully operational, explain their status, what additional steps remain to be completed, and when such final steps will be taken.

b To what extent have you used, or do you plan to use, contributions as an endowment fund, i.e., hold contributions to produce income for the support of your exempt activities?

8 Will any of the organization's facilities be managed by another organization or individual under a contractual agreement? . . . . ☐ Yes ☐ No
If "Yes," attach a copy of each contract and explain the relationship between the applicant and each of the other parties.

Figure 1–3 APPLICATION FOR RECOGNITION OF EXEMPTION (continued)

Part III Activities and Operational Information (Continued)

9 a Have the recipients been required or will they be required to pay for the organization's benefits, services, or products? . . . . . ☐ Yes ☐ No
If "Yes," explain and show how the charges are determined.

b Does or will the organization limit its benefits, services, or products to specific classes of individuals? . . . . ☐ Yes ☐ No
If "Yes," explain how the recipients or beneficiaries are or will be selected.

10 Is the organization a membership organization? . . . . . ☐ Yes ☐ No
If "Yes," complete the following:

a Describe the organization's membership requirements and attach a schedule of membership fees and dues.

b Describe your present and proposed efforts to attract members, and attach a copy of any descriptive literature or promotional material used for this purpose.

c Are benefits, services, or products limited to members? . . . . . ☐ Yes ☐ No
If "No," explain.

11 Does or will the organization engage in activities tending to influence legislation or intervene in any way in political campaigns? . . . . . ☐ Yes ☐ No
If "Yes," explain. (**Note:** *You may wish to file* ***Form 5768****, Election/Revocation of Election by an Eligible Section 501(c)(3) Organization to Make Expenditures to Influence Legislation.*)

12 Does the organization have a pension plan for employees? . . . . . ☐ Yes ☐ No

13 a Are you filing Form 1023 within 15 months from the end of the month in which you were created or formed as required by section 508(a) and the related regulations? (See General Instructions.). . . . . ☐ Yes ☐ No

b If you answer "No," to 13a and you claim that you fit an exception to the notice requirements under section 508(a), attach an explanation of your basis for the claimed exception.

c If you answer "No," to 13a and section 508(a) does apply to you, you may be eligible for relief under regulations section 1.9100 from the application of section 508(a). Do you wish to request relief? . . . . . ☐ Yes ☐ No

d If you answer "Yes," to 13c, attach a detailed statement that satisfies the requirements of Rev. Proc. 79-63.

e If you answer "No," to both 13a and 13c and section 508(a) does apply to you, your qualification as a section 501(c)(3) organization can be recognized only from the date this application is filed with your key District Director. Therefore, do you want us to consider your application as a request for recognition of exemption as a section 501(c)(3) organization from the date the application is received and not retroactively to the date you were formed (see instructions)? . . . . . ☐ Yes ☐ No

Part IV Statement as to Private Foundation Status (see instructions)

1 Is the organization a private foundation? . . . . . ☐ Yes ☐ No

2 If you answer "Yes," to question 1 and the organization claims to be a private operating foundation, check here ► ☐ and complete Part VII.

3 If you answer "No," to question 1, indicate the type of ruling you are requesting regarding the organization's status under section 509 by checking the box(es) below that apply:

a Definitive ruling under section 509(a)(1), (2), (3), or (4) ► ☐. Complete Part VI.

b Advance ruling under ► ☐ sections 509(a)(1) and 170(b)(1)(A)(vi) or ► ☐ section 509(a)(2)—see instructions.

(**Note:** *If you want an advance ruling, you* ***must*** *complete and attach two Forms 872-C to the application.*)

Part V Financial Data

Statement of Support, Revenue, and Expenses for the period beginning ...., 19 ...., and ending ...., 19 ....

Note: *Complete the financial statements for the current year and for each of the three years immediately before it. If in existence less than four years, complete the statements for each year in existence.* ***If in existence less than one year, also provide proposed budgets for the two years following the current year.***

Section	Line	Description		Line no.	Amount
Support and Revenue	1	Gross contributions, gifts, grants, and similar amounts received		1	
	2	Gross dues and assessments of members		2	
	3 a	Gross amounts derived from activities related to organization's exempt purpose (attach schedule)			
	b	Minus cost of sales		3c	
	4 a	Gross amounts from unrelated business activities (attach schedule)			
	b	Minus cost of sales		4c	
	5 a	Gross amount received from sale of assets, excluding inventory items (attach schedule)			
	b	Minus cost or other basis and sales expenses of assets sold		5c	
	6	Investment income (see instructions)		6	
	7	Other revenue (attach schedule)		7	
	8	**Total support and revenue**		8	
Expenses	9	Fundraising expenses		9	
	10	Contributions, gifts, grants, and similar amounts paid (attach schedule)		10	
	11	Disbursements to or for benefit of members (attach schedule)		11	
	12	Compensation of officers, directors, and trustees (attach schedule)		12	
	13	Other salaries and wages		13	
	14	Interest		14	
	15	Rent		15	
	16	Depreciation and depletion		16	
	17	Other (attach schedule)		17	
	18	**Total expenses**		18	
	19	Excess of support and revenue over expenses (line 8 minus line 18)		19	

Balance Sheet
(at the end of the period shown above)

	Assets		
20	Cash: a Interest bearing accounts	20a	
	b Other	20b	
21	Accounts receivable, net	21	
22	Inventories	22	
23	Bonds and notes (attach schedule)	23	
24	Corporate stocks (attach schedule)	24	
25	Mortgage loans (attach schedule)	25	
26	Other investments (attach schedule)	26	
27	Depreciable and depletable assets (attach schedule)	27	
28	Land	28	
29	Other assets (attach schedule)	29	
30	**Total assets**	30	
	Liabilities		
31	Accounts payable	31	
32	Contributions, gifts, grants, etc., payable	32	
33	Mortgages and notes payable (attach schedule)	33	
34	Other liabilities (attach schedule)	34	
35	**Total liabilities**	35	
	Fund Balances or Net Worth		
36	Total fund balances or net worth	36	
37	**Total liabilities and fund balances or net worth** (line 35 plus line 36)	37	

If there has been any substantial change in any aspect of your financial activities since the period shown above ended, check the box and attach a detailed explanation . . . ☐

Part VI Non-Private Foundation Status (Definitive ruling only) (Continued)

B.—Analysis of Financial Support (Continued)

13 If the organization's non-private foundation status is based on:

a Sections 509(a)(1) and 170(b)(1)(A)(iv) or (vi).—Attach a list showing the name and amount contributed by each person (other than a governmental unit or "publicly supported" organization) whose total gifts for the entire period were more than the amount shown on line 11.

b Section 509(a)(2).—For each of the years included on lines 1, 2, and 3, attach a list showing the name of and amount received from each person who is a "disqualified person."

For each of the years on line 3, attach a list showing the name of and amount received from each payor (other than a "disqualified person") whose payments to the organization were more than $5,000. For this purpose, "payor" includes, but is not limited to, any organization described in sections 170(b)(1)(A)(i) through (vi) and any governmental agency or bureau.

C.—Supplemental Information Concerning Organizations Claiming Non-Private Foundation Status Under Section 509(a)(3)

1 Organizations supported by applicant organization: Name and address of supported organization	Has the supported organization received a ruling or determination letter that it is not a private foundation by reason of section 509(a)(1) or (2)?
	☐ Yes ☐ No
	☐ Yes ☐ No
	☐ Yes ☐ No
	☐ Yes ☐ No
	☐ Yes ☐ No

2 To what extent are the members of your governing board elected or appointed by the supported organization(s)?

3 What is the extent of common supervision or control that you and the supported organization(s) share?

4 To what extent do(es) the supported organization(s) have a significant voice in your investment policies, the making and timing of grants, and in otherwise directing the use of your income or assets?

5 Does the mentioning of the supported organization(s) in your governing instrument make you a trust that the supported organization(s) can enforce under State law and compel to make an accounting? . . . . ☐ Yes ☐ No
If "Yes," explain.

6 What portion of your income do you pay to each supported organization and how significant is the support to each?

7 To what extent do you conduct activities that would otherwise be carried out by the supported organization(s)? Explain why these activities would otherwise be carried on by the supported organization(s).

8 Is the applicant organization controlled directly or indirectly by one or more "disqualified persons" (other than one who is a disqualified person solely because he or she is a manager) or by an organization which is not described in section 509(a)(1) or (2)? . . . . ☐ Yes ☐ No
If "Yes," explain.

Form 1023 (Rev. 3-86) Page **8**

Part VII Basis for Status as a Private Operating Foundation

If the organization claims to be an operating foundation described in section 4942(j)(3) and—

(a) bases its claim to private operating foundation status on normal and regular operations over a period of years; or

(b) is newly created, set up as a private operating foundation, and has at least one year's experience;

provide the information under the income test and under one of the three supplemental tests (assets, endowment, or support). If the organization does not have at least one year's experience, complete line 21. If the organization's private operating foundation status depends on its normal and regular operations as described in (a) above, attach a schedule similar to the one below showing the data in tabular form for the three years next preceding the most recent tax year. (See regulations section 53.4942(b)-1 for additional information before completing the "Income Test" section of Part VII.) Organizations claiming section 4942(j)(5) status must satisfy the income test and the endowment test.

Income Test		**Most recent tax year**
1a Adjusted net income, as defined in regulations section 53.4942(a)-2(d)	1a	
b Minimum investment return, as defined in regulations section 53.4942(a)-2(c)	1b	
2 Qualifying distributions:		
a Amounts (including administrative expenses) paid directly for the active conduct of the activities for which organized and operated under section 501(c)(3)(attach schedule)	2a	
b Amounts paid to acquire assets to be used (or held for use) directly in carrying out purposes described in sections 170(c)(1) or 170(c)(2)(B) (attach schedule)	2b	
c Amounts set aside for specific projects that are for purposes described in section 170(c)(1) or 170(c)(2)(B) (attach schedule)	2c	
d Total qualifying distributions (add lines 2a, b, and c)	2d	
3 Percentages:		
a Percentage of qualifying distributions to adjusted net income (divide line 2d by line 1a)	3a	%
b Percentage of qualifying distributions to minimum investment return (divide line 2d by line 1b) (Percentage must be at least 85% for 3a or 3b)	3b	%
Assets Test		
4 Value of organization's assets used in activities that directly carry out the exempt purposes. Do not include assets held merely for investment or production of income (attach schedule)	4	
5 Value of any stock of a corporation that is controlled by applicant organization and carries out its exempt purposes (attach statement describing corporation)	5	
6 Value of all qualifying assets (add lines 4 and 5)	6	
7 Value of applicant organization's total assets	7	
8 Percentage of qualifying assets to total assets (divide line 6 by line 7—percentage must exceed 65%)	8	%
Endowment Test		
9 Value of assets not used (or held for use) directly in carrying out exempt purposes:		
a Monthly average of investment securities at fair market value	9a	
b Monthly average of cash balances	9b	
c Fair market value of all other investment property (attach schedule)	9c	
d Total (add lines 9a, b, and c)	9d	
10 Subtract acquisition indebtedness related to line 9 items (attach schedule)	10	
11 Balance (subtract line 10 from line 9d)	11	
12 Multiply line 11 by 3⅓% (⅔ of the percentage for the minimum investment return computation under section 4942(e)). Line 2d above must equal or exceed the result of this computation	12	
Support Test		
13 Applicant organization's support as defined in section 509(d)	13	
14 Subtract amount of gross investment income as defined in section 509(e)	14	
15 Support for purposes of section 4942(j)(3)(B)(iii) (subtract line 14 from line 13)	15	
16 Support received from the general public, five or more exempt organizations, or a combination of these sources (attach schedule)	16	
17 For persons (other than exempt organizations) contributing more than 1% of line 15, enter the total amounts that are more than 1% of line 15	17	
18 Subtract line 17 from line 16	18	
19 Percentage of total support (divide line 18 by line 15—must be at least 85%)	19	%

20 Does line 16 include support from an exempt organization that is more than 25% of the amount of line 15? ☐ Yes ☐ No

21 Newly created organizations with less than one year's experience: Attach a statement explaining how the organization is planning to satisfy the requirements of section 4942(j)(3) for the income test and one of the supplemental tests during its first year's operation. Include a description of plans and arrangements, press clippings, public announcements, solicitations for funds, etc.

Part VIII Required Schedules for Special Activities

	If "Yes," check here	And complete schedule—
1 Is the organization, or any part of it, a school?		A
2 Does the organization provide or administer any scholarship benefits, student aid, etc.?		B
3 Has the organization taken over, or will it take over, the facilities of a "for profit" institution?		C
4 Is the organization, or any part of it, a hospital or medical research organization?		D
5 Is the organization, or any part of it, a home for the aged?		E
6 Is the organization, or any part of it, a litigating organization (public interest law firm or similar organization)?		F
7 Is the organization, or any part of it, formed to promote amateur sports competition?		G

Schedule A.—Schools, Colleges, and Universities

1 Is the organization an instrumentality of a State or political subdivision of a State? ☐ Yes ☐ No
If "Yes," document this in Part III and do not complete items 2 through 9 of this schedule. (See instructions for Schedule A.)

2 Does or will the organization (or any department or division within it) discriminate in any way on the basis of race with respect to:

- **a** Admissions? ☐ Yes ☐ No
- **b** Use of facilities or exercise of student privileges? ☐ Yes ☐ No
- **c** Faculty or administrative staff? ☐ Yes ☐ No
- **d** Scholarship or loan program? ☐ Yes ☐ No

If "Yes," for any of the above, explain.

3 Does the organization include a statement in its charter, bylaws, or other governing instrument, or in a resolution of its governing body, that it has a racially nondiscriminatory policy as to students? ☐ Yes ☐ No
Attach whatever corporate resolutions or other official statements the organization has made on this subject.

4 a Has the organization made its racially nondiscriminatory policies known in a manner that brings the policies to the attention of all segments of the general community which its serves? ☐ Yes ☐ No
If "Yes," describe how these policies have been publicized and state the frequency with which relevant notices or announcements have been made. If no newspaper or broadcast media notices have been used, explain.

b If applicable, attach clippings of any relevant newspaper notices or advertising, or copies of tapes or scripts used for media broadcasts. Also attach copies of brochures and catalogues dealing with student admissions, programs, and scholarships, as well as representative copies of all written advertising used as a means of informing prospective students of your programs.

5 Attach a numerical schedule showing the racial composition, as of the current academic year, and projected as far as may be feasible for the next academic year, of: (a) the student body, (b) the faculty and administrative staff.

6 Attach a list showing the amount of any scholarship and loan funds awarded to students enrolled and the racial composition of the students who have received the awards.

7 a Attach a list of the organization's incorporators, founders, board members, and donors of land or buildings, whether individuals or organizations.

b State whether any of the organizations listed in **a** have as an objective the maintenance of segregated public or private school education, and, if so, whether any of the individuals listed in **a** are officers or active members of such organizations.

8 Indicate the public school district and county in which the organization is located.

9 Has the organization ever been determined by a State or Federal administrative agency or judicial body to be racially discriminatory? ☐ Yes ☐ No
If "Yes," attach a detailed explanation identifying the parties to the suit, the forum in which the case was heard, the cause of action, the holding in the case, and the citations (if any) for the case. Also describe in detail what changes in your operation, if any, have occurred since then.

Schedule B.—Organizations Providing Scholarship Benefits, Student Aid, etc. to Individuals

1 a Describe the nature of the scholarship benefit, student aid, etc., including the terms and conditions governing its use, whether a gift or a loan, and the amount. If the organization has established or will establish several categories of scholarship benefits, identify each kind of benefit and explain how the organization determines the recipients for each category. Attach a sample copy of any application the organization requires or will require of individuals to be considered for scholarship grants, loans, or similar benefits. (Private foundations that make grants for travel, study or other similar purposes are required to obtain advance approval of scholarship procedures. See regulations sections 53.4945-4(c) and (d).)

b If you want this application considered as a request for approval of grant procedures in the event we determine that you are a private foundation, check here . . . . . ▶ ☐

2 What limitations or restrictions are there on the class of individuals who are eligible recipients? Specifically explain whether there are, or will be, any restrictions or limitations in the selection procedures based upon race and whether there are, or will be, restrictions or limitations in selection procedures based on the employment status of the prospective recipient or any relative of the prospective recipient. Also indicate the approximate number of eligible individuals.

3 Indicate the number of grants you anticipate making annually . . . . .

4 List the names, addresses, duties, and relevant background of the members of your selection committee. If you base your selections in any way on the employment status of the applicant or any relative of the applicant, indicate whether there is or has been any direct or indirect relationship between the members of the selection committee and the employer. Also indicate whether relatives of the members of the selection committee are possible recipients or have been recipients.

5 Describe any procedures you have for supervising grants (such as obtaining reports or transcripts) that you award, and any procedures you have for taking action if the terms of the grant are violated.

SCHEDULE C.—Successors to "For Profit" Institutions

1 What was the name of the predecessor organization and the nature of its activities?

2 Who were the owners or principal stockholders of the predecessor organization? (If more space is needed, attach schedule.)

Name and address	Share or interest

(continued on next page)

Figure 1–4

CRITERIA FOR DEVELOPING PROGRAM PHILOSOPHY*

1. What is the scope of the program? Who is served? What geographic area is served? What are the ages of the children served?

2. What is the mission of the program? What are its chief purposes—education, child care, parenting education?

3. Are any unique needs addressed by the program? For example, are bilingual or children with handicapping conditions served by the program?

4. Which theories of early childhood education or educational schools of thought guide the program? How do these theories influence the program or curriculum? Cite source of theories wherever possible.

5. What principles of early childhood education guide the program and the work of teaching or caregiving staff, administrators, and support staff? What are the essential elements of:
   - **a.** the learning environment;
   - **b.** staff-child interactions;
   - **c.** programming for children;
   - **d.** parental involvement?

---

*Philosophical statements should be short and concise.

Figure 1–5

SAMPLE PROGRAM PHILOSOPHY*

I. Statement of Program Philosophy

The Philadelphia Parent-Child Center was founded in 1968 by a small group of parents concerned about the developmental needs and education of their infants and toddlers. The Learning Center component of the Parent-Child Center provides a supportive environment in which both parent and child benefit. The Learning Center operates in half-day sessions, four days per week. Trained early childhood educators, working together with parents, offer a program of activities designed to facilitate the physical, cognitive, and psychosocial development of children eighteen months to three years of age.

II. Principles of Child Development

The Learning Center program and curriculum are guided by the following principles of child development:

A. **Physical Development.** Physical development proceeds according to a predetermined sequence and at a rate that is individual for each child. The rate of a child's physical growth may be enhanced or slowed by the environments to which the child is regularly exposed and also by the extent of the development-facilitative skills possessed by the adults who influence the child's life. Physical development may be impaired by the circumstances of a child's birth or by the condition of the child's health when he or she is born; that is, by the presence of birth defects or environmental hazards. Unfortunately, many such problems are not apparent at birth; instead, they only become evident as the child becomes older and fails to meet developmental norms.

Adults wishing to facilitate children's development must regularly plot the course of each child's growth in order to determine that this growth is on target. These adults must also determine the types of developmental support needed by each child, planning both individual (one child to one adult) and group activities to meet those needs. Where delay or impairment of physical development is evident, the cause of the problem must be determined and an individualized prescription developed and followed to enable the child to reach his or her maximum potential.

---

*Kathleen Pullan Watkins, "Learning Center Curriculum" (Philadelphia, PA: Philadelphia Parent-Child Center, 1988). Reprinted by permission.

The physical development of the eighteen-month-old child includes the ability to walk and run for short distances. This movement is usually awkward and ungainly due to the disproportionate nature of the toddler body. This child can build a short block tower and can paint and draw using random lines or squiggles (scribbling). Although the eighteen-month-old does not have a great deal of flexibility in fingers or wrists, he or she can also remove shoes, hat, and mittens and unzip a large zipper.

The twenty-four month old is developing greater flexibility of movement. When walking or running this child leans forward slightly, a more natural posture for this activity at this age. The ability to kick a large ball has now developed, and both hands are used in unison for activities such as opening a door. This child enjoys taking apart simple toys and putting them together again; for example, stacking rings or nesting blocks.

At thirty months, the fine-motor skills of the child continue to improve. This child can turn pages when looking at a book, provided the pages are of sufficient weight. The thirty-month-old child enjoys a variety of media, such as easel and finger painting, clay, sand, and water, for creative expression. The child's wrists are no longer as stiff or inflexible. The thirty-month old is also a climber and jumper where small heights are involved, enjoying outdoor equipment made for these purposes.

The artwork of the three year old begins to show the use of designs; that is, the use of shapes and lines together. This is an indicator of even greater flexibility of fine-motor movement. Eye-hand coordination shows similar improvement at this time, although much additional practice is required to refine these skills. The three year old also continues to enjoy block building; however, blocks are often combined with other toys at this age to facilitate dramatic play themes.

A great many additional physical skills develop during the toddler years. While this document does not provide a complete summary of them, it does show some of the highlights of this period.

B. Cognitive Development. According to the late child-development theorist Jean Piagét, the toddler (eighteen months to three years of age) is at either the sensorimotor or preoperational stage of cognitive development. The child who is at the earlier (sensorimotor) phase is characterized by egocentric thinking. He or she is unable to see situations from the points of view of others. Experiences are interpreted in a very subjective manner, based primarily on the child's own concrete experiences. For example, all men the child meets are likely to be called "daddy"; even male teachers and caregivers.

The sensorimotor child is also an intensely curious explorer, still actively engaged in the process of discovering the power that he or she has over the environment and even over his or her own body. For this reason, eighteen-month olds may repeatedly seek out or touch items that are interesting to them, no matter how many times they may be warned away from those things that may be harmful to them. The child tends to be focused on cause-and-effect relationships (the response that comes from some action that he or she performs). The warnings and rules of adults are quickly forgotten in an effort to repeat something interesting or find out how something works.

During the last phases of the sensorimotor period, the child also experiments with a variety of means to achieve the same end result. This is yet another reason for the seemingly endless stream of repetitive behaviors during the toddler years.

Sometimes to the surprise of parents, many toddlers are still suprisingly oral during this stage. They often continue to enjoy a bottle or pacifier, or mouthing toys, and they may chew on blankets or other familiar objects. While not always the most sanitary means of learning, these activities provide a great deal of information to the developing child. Information on taste, texture, and smell are but three of the types of sensorial learning that arise from sucking, biting, and chewing.

During the preoperational phase of cognitive development, beginning at approximately age two, there are a number of new characteristics observable in the toddler, although the child's thinking continues to be egocentric.

Understanding the reasoning or feelings of others may be difficult or impossible for the two or three year old. In addition, the child often attributes the characteristics of living things to those things which are inanimate or nonliving. Called *animism,* this characteristic is responsible for the child's belief that dolls have feelings like those of people, or even that weeping willow trees really cry.

One genuine drawback to this and similar characteristics of the preoperational stage is that the child may literally believe everything he or she hears. Stories or movies about ghosts, witches, dinosaurs, and superheroes are often the source of more childhood nightmares than pleasures.

Preoperational-stage children may also be confused about many aspects of time (temporal relations). Any parent who has taken a long drive with a child only to be asked repeatedly, "Are we there yet?" has some conception of this problem. The toddler (and preschooler) do not understand terms like *yesterday, tomorrow, year, month,* or *week.* Told about dinosaurs that lived millions of years ago, the child may feel certain that a dinosaur will come to his room at night and eat him.

These are but a few of the many cognitive characteristics and changes taking place during the toddler period. Understanding of the young child's thinking is an essential tool to be used by adults in facilitating the child's growth.

C. **Language Development.** One development that proceeds at a very rapid pace during toddlerhood is that of language and communication skills. By eighteen months of age, a normally developing child says about ten recognizable words, although some children may say many more. Eighteen-month-old children will also talk or sing to themselves, generally when they think they are unobserved. With coaxing, some eighteen-month-olds will join adults in familiar songs, but many children this age are shy and will watch as adults sing.

A child this age understands many of the simple things that adults say to him or her. Understood vocabulary (called *receptive* vocabulary) is always greater in humans than that vocabulary that becomes a part of our own speech patterns (called *expressive* vocabulary). The eighteen-month-old can follow simple commands such as "Bring me that blanket" or "Get your coat." This child may tend, however, to express his or her own ideas with a single word. "Go" may mean "Can I go with you?" or "Please don't go." Of course, when tired the very young child may resort to crying or whining to express needs.

By twenty-four months of age, the muscles of the mouth, tongue, lips, and larynx have developed in a way that permits the child to articulate more clearly. This child speaks in short, two- or three-word sentences and enjoys conversing with adults and playing with the telephone. It is not unusual today for children who have had exposure to articulate parents, television and movies, and preschool experience to have a high degree of skill with language by twenty-four months of age. A significant development, related to the child's cognitive growth, is the newly developed ability to generalize. No longer are all women "mommy"; some are now "girls" or "ladies" or "women."

By thirty months, the child has a genuine appreciation of songs and stories. To the surprise (or annoyance) of some adults, the child often wants to hear the same familiar story over and over. Gradually, the child begins mouthing or repeating those parts of the tale that he or she is familiar with. When a particular commercial or show theme is heard on the television, many children will sing along. Language is beginning to be a real tool for communication. The breadth of possibilities for language are beginning to be apparent to the child.

By this time, children usually enjoy looking at books and magazines alone, particularly the pictures. When read to by an adult, they may want to name the objects or people in the pictures, often remembering in detail what grown-ups have told them. It is during this time that children begin to show a sense of humor, laughing spontaneously at the behavior of others, at television antics, even at pets. At this age the child's vocabulary is developing at an extraordinarily rapid rate; he or she may be learning hundreds of new words per day.

By age three the child is using language as a tool to express imagination. He or she imitates adults, friends, superheroes, and characters from favorite stories. Extremely interested in new words, the child's vocabulary continues the rapid pace begun at the end of the first year. Most three year olds listen and respond well to adult attempts to reason with them. The ability is now present to understand and even use some terms related to time and measurement, such as *here, there, now, under,* and *over.*

D. Psychosocial Development. Psychoanalyst Erik Erikson speaks of the toddler period in terms of the growth of two crucial social-emotional skills, autonomy and initiative. As children begin to develop self-help skills such as feeding, toileting, and dressing, they need the encouragement and support of the adults in their lives. As they gradually begin to move out of the protective circle formed by the family and begin a series of lifelong experiments with new people and experiences, they need to have opportunities for success and rewards along the way. While success is not always possible or even desirable, some realization of goals is essential to the development of a healthy sense of self. Sometimes parents need assistance to recognize that allowing a child to win some parent-child conflicts does not rob the parent of influence in the child's life. Throughout this period, adults who interact with children must consistently express their pleasure in the child's efforts and approval of the child's persistence.

At eighteen months of age, most children are still very obviously attached to their parents. While some separations may continue to be difficult up until four years of age or beyond, those children who begin attending a preschool or nursery program in infancy usually make a rapid adjustment to school life. Nonetheless, the eighteen to thirty-six month old can be "clingy" and demand a great deal of attention when left at school by parents.

In part because the toddler is so very egocentric at this age, group activities are often not very successful. The child does not have a grasp of the give and take aspects of human relationships. While adults encourage children to share, take turns, and otherwise cooperate with one another, these are not concepts that the toddler understands. The eighteen month-old is often extremely possessive of adults and personal objects. The mere interest of another child in a special toy can produce a temper tantrum and screams of "Mine, mine!" The toddler may still cling to a doll, teddy bear, or blanket. When tired or hungry he or she is not able to express personal needs and may cry or even withdraw. This behavior generally persists through the toddler stage, ending gradually as the child enters the preschool period.

By age three there have been significant changes in the child's ability to interact with others. A child this age is intensely interested in other children and sometimes even has the ability to show empathy for others. The three year old demonstrates preferences in food and clothing and may object strenuously to what he or she does not like. Three year olds show pride in accomplishments and possessions such as new shoes or barrettes, but may not yet share things easily with others. When tired the three year old sometimes reverts to babyish behavior.

Although steady psychosocial development does not proceed at the same pace as physical, cognitive, or language development, it is psychosocial development, that is perhaps most dramatically influenced by early experiences with parents and other caregivers.

E. **Summary.** The Learning Center staff recognizes that development in the physical, cognitive, language, and psychosocial areas occurs at a predictable and yet highly individualized rate. Development in one area does not necessarily keep pace with that in other areas. For example, the child who is cognitively advanced may be delayed in his or her social-emotional development. The child who has superior physical development may be of normal intelligence.

The Learning Center staff also understands that a crucial role of this program is to recognize instances of developmental delay in young children. When a delay in a developmental area is suspected, symptoms are recorded and verified and referral is made to the proper health care personnel or agency for diagnosis and treatment. This is the role of the health services component of the Philadelphia Parent-Child Center.

The staff of the Learning Center is concerned with the development of the whole child. Since there is no single theory of child development that attempts to explain all aspects of development, the approach taken in this developmental program is eclectic. That is, it includes the predominant theories in all major areas of development and adheres to the philosophy that the best approach for young children and their families is one that provides for success experiences for the children, their families, and staff.

III. **Principles of Early Childhood Education**

The Learning Center program and curriculum are guided by the following principles of early childhood education:

A. **Learning Environment.** It is the philosophy of the Learning Center that a chief ingredient in the learning experience of young children is the preparation of the environment in which they spend a large percentage of time. The environment is prepared in such a way that as the child interacts within it, he or she is prompted toward sensory experiences, experimentation, and arrival at conceptual conclusions. It takes considerable time and effort on the part of teachers to plan such an environment. Teachers must be aware of the developmental needs of children, as these needs pertain to both the individual and the group. Teachers must recognize that these needs change constantly, and the prepared environment, to reflect those changes, must be neither boring nor overstimulating to the child.

The environment of the Learning Center contains the following elements to meet the needs of toddlers:

1. *Child-sized equipment*—to promote the children's comfort and ease of movement within the classroom
2. *Sensory materials*—to facilitate the growth of tactile, visual, olfactory, and auditory skills
3. *Fine-motor materials*—to promote the growth of hand skills and eye-hand coordination
4. *Gross-motor materials*—to facilitate the development of large muscle-group skills
5. *Language arts materials*—to promote listening, speaking, and prewriting skills
6. *Social studies materials*—to promote self-recognition and awareness, awareness of family and community, social skills, dramatic play, and nurturant behaviors
7. *Premathematics materials*—to facilitate knowledge of numbers, time, sequence, measurement, and shape
8. *Materials for creative expression* (art, music, and drama)—to promote creative self-expression and appreciation of the creativity of others

B. **Staff-Child Interactions.** The staff members of the Learning Center recognize the critical nature of their relationship with the toddlers in the program. The teachers are seen as facilitators rather than as directors, of children's learning. Other roles of teachers at the Learning Center are those of:

1. *Observer*—to chart development, to be aware of nondevelopmental changes that influence the well-being of the children
2. *Nurturer*—to provide for the social and emotional needs of children away from home
3. *Role model*—to inspire the imitation of language and social skills as yet unacquired by the children

4. *Limit setter*—to help the children harness and use energy constructively in both classroom and outdoor environments
5. *Goal facilitator*—to identify the goals appropriate for each child and plan the environment and curriculum to help the child achieve those aims
6. *Activity planner*—to develop and schedule activities in a way beneficial to the physical, cognitive, and psychosocial development of the child and the group
7. *Mediator*—to help bridge communication gaps as these arise between the children or the children and adults
8. *Advocate*—to speak out for the rights and needs of the individual child or the group, whether to teaching staff, the child's family, or to community representatives

C. **Programming.** The Learning Center has a child-centered rather than an adult-directed program. The program is based on sound principles of child development and early childhood education. The significance of child-centeredness is that the children, and their development and individual needs, provide the basis for planning the daily program, for scheduling, and for the content of the curriculum. As the staff plans for children, the following are among the considerations:

1. The status of the individual child's growth and development based on developmental assessment
2. The general developmental level of each group of children
3. The interests of individual children and of children in this age group
4. The materials and equipment available in the classroom and outdoors
5. Upcoming holidays and special events, and their significance to the children and their families
6. The season of the year, prevailing weather conditions, and how these affect children
7. The mood of the children on a given day
8. The activity level of the children during various seasons and at different times of the day
9. Skills and special interests of the staff
10. Available community resources

11. Special concerns of and goals that parents have for their children

12. Skills children will need for success in the Head Start program and in later school experiences

D. Home-School Relations and Parental Involvement. The Learning Center is a program deeply committed to working with the whole family. A primary purpose of the program is to provide education for the parents as well as the child. Toward this end, the involvement of parents is mandated at the 50 percent level, a figure expected to rise to 100 percent participation in the future.

Parental involvement takes a variety of forms. Parents may elect to volunteer their services in the classroom. Parent volunteers receive training enabling them to function in positive and constructive ways with children. Parental assistance is valued during daily routines, such as feeding and toileting, and also during the preparation for and performance of daily activities.

Parent volunteers also accompany staff and children on walks and trips. Extra pairs of adult hands help teachers maximize child safety while children are away from the center. Parent volunteers also help facilitate the learning derived by children from new or novel experiences encountered outside the center.

Parent training is another important aspect of parental involvement at the Learning Center. Parents regularly receive information on a broad range of child-care and childrearing topics from specialists in a variety of areas. Participation in some training events is also mandatory for parents. However, not all training is formalized. The staff of the Learning Center sees all encounters with parents as opportunities to exchange information about children and support the needs of developing families.

The coordinator of parental involvement plays a role crucial in the home-school relationship. This individual schedules and conducts orientation for new parents in order to acquaint them with the Learning Center program, and its policies and procedures. Through the parental involvement coordinator, parents first become familiar with the scope of the program and their responsibilities within it. The coordinator also serves as the link between the parents and the Parent-Child Center agency. He or she advises parents of upcoming trips and other special events in which parental involvement is encouraged. The parental involvement coordinator is also a gatherer of information about resources both inside and outside of the agency. He or she helps to assure that families in need are connected with the social-service personnel or facilities designed to assist parents with problems.

Home visits are another element of the Learning Center's parental involvement component. Staff members make regular visits to children's homes, where information about individual children and about the program may be exchanged with parents.

The relationship between staff and parents is believed to be of vital importance to the child's development. When interacting with or planning involvement with parents, staff members bear in mind the degree of their impact on families. They demonstrate the value of the parent-teacher relationship by acknowledging:

- The influence of the parent on the developing child
- The importance of the family's goals for the child
- The lifestyle of each family
- The unique beliefs and value system of each family
- The family's ethnic, cultural, and religious background
- The desire of parents to learn about their children
- The pride parents take in their children and their children's accomplishments
- The unique styles of childrearing practiced within each family
- The value of parental input into and contributions to the Learning Center program
- The confidentiality of family information

E. **Summary.** The principles of early childhood education adopted by the Learning Center are a collaboration of accepted practices in the field. The concept of the prepared environment is derived from the principles of Maria Montessori, renowned theorist and developer of curriculum for early childhood programs. Montessori saw the learning environment as a key ingredient in the child's learning. She also felt that a chief role of the teacher is to plan and "prepare" the environment for the child's interaction with it, creating a place where the child teaches him- or herself and the teacher becomes a facilitator.

Figure 1–5 SAMPLE PROGRAM PHILOSOPHY (continued)

The staff-child relationship at the Learning Center also has its basis in the Montessori philosophy. Montessori called her teachers *directors,* because she saw them as conductors of learning. The teacher prepares the environment and encourages children to use the techniques and freedom provided to explore that space. The Montessori teacher is also a keen observer of children, aware of the approach of new phases of development and ready to respond to them. As a guide to children's learning, the Learning Center teacher urges and supports but does not force children toward learning or participation in any activity.

Other aspects of the teacher-child relationship at the Learning Center are influenced by a growing body of research on the needs of toddlers and the roles of the caregiver/teacher. One such study indicates that high-quality toddler programs have caregivers that provide the young child with a "sense of security and enjoyment of social exchange"; that they promote the child's sense of self-worth; and that they promote the development of a secure attachment relationship with one or two special caregivers. It is this type of teacher-child interaction that is valued and practiced at the Learning Center.

The child-centeredness of the Learning Center program is strongly tied to the model of progressive education first advocated by John Dewey and later by the proponents of "open education." Dewey believed that teachers should be planners and correlators of the curriculum content. He felt that a unit approach to teaching should be employed and a problem-solving approach to learning should be utilized. Through an open-ended style of presentation of information, children are urged to explore, question, and seek their own answers to problems.

Alene Auerbach has identified a series of principles to be observed by teachers working with parents. She says that parents care about their children, and want to and can learn about them. Auerbach believes that these assumptions about parents are the cornerstone of the home-school relationship. More recently, Carol Gestwicki, author of *Home, School and Community Relations: A Guide to Working with Parents,* has urged the development of parent-teacher partnerships through frequent communication and support by teachers for the parenting role. This is the type of relationship sought with families at the Learning Center.

Figure 1–6

CRITERIA FOR DEVELOPING PROGRAM POLICIES*

I. **Admission Policies for Children**

A. Making application (how a parent applies)

B. The admission interview (when conducted; what the interview consists of)

C. Developmental history (taken at the admission interview)

D. Health Appraisal (a physician's exam required for admission)

E. Immunization record (required for admission)

F. Placement on the waiting list for admission (circumstances under which this occurs; how long a name remains on the list; how notification of an opening is made)

G. Admission procedures (how the child is admitted; what the child's schedule is during the first week of admittance)

H. Attendance requirements and penalities for failure to attend regularly (where applicable)

II. **Fees and Payment Policies (where applicable)**

A. Fee schedule (for programs with sliding-scale payments)

B. Fee due dates; how payment may be made (check, money order, cash, etc.); penalties for late payment

C. Arrangement of fees for family holidays, child illness, two or more siblings in program

D. Fees due after departure from program (collection policies)

III. **Calendar of Program Openings and Closings**

IV. **Policies Governing Ill/Sick Children**

A. Child ill upon arrival at school

B. Child becoming ill at school

C. Isolation of ill children

D. Administration of medication

E. Children with AIDS and other infectious diseases

F. Emergency notification information

*Other policies may address staff recruitment, qualifications, hiring, and firing.

Figure 1–6 CRITERIA FOR DEVELOPING PROGRAM POLICIES (continued)

V. Accident Policies

A. Accident response procedures
B. Emergency notification of parents
C. Treatment of injuries
D. Hospitalization of a child
E. Accident report procedures

VI. Child Abuse and Neglect Policies

A. Procedures for suspected abuse or neglect
B. Documentation of suspected abuse or neglect
C. Reporting procedures for suspected abuse and neglect

VII. Discipline Policies (see Figure 1–7)

A. Guidelines for staff/parent interaction with children
B. Acceptable ways of disciplining children
C. Roles of parents in the discipline process

VIII. Other Responsibilities of Parents

A. Children's clothing (appropriate for weather; extra set required)
B. Children's food (snack and meal suggestions, where applicable)
C. Bedding (washing required weekly when children nap at center)
D. Pick up and delivery of children (must be timely; cannot be by unauthorized persons)
E. Center notification in event of child's extended absence due to illness or family vacation, in event of family problems affecting child, in event of at-home accident or injury to child
F. Policies about toys and supplies children bring to school

IX. Grievance Policies for Parents and Staff

A. Grievance hierarchy (who to talk to first, second)
B. Recourse for unresolved problems

Figure 1–7

SAMPLE DISCIPLINE POLICIES*

The Learning Center operates on the premise that young children are never "bad." The types of inappropriate behavior most often seen in toddler-age children (including temper tantrums, refusal to cooperate, hitting other children, and failure to follow rules) are usually the result of the child's level of development. A toddler simply lacks the social-emotional, cognitive, and physical skills to comply with many adult demands. For these reasons the Learning Center staff uses the following guidelines for promoting positive behavior and for responding to problem behavior.

At the Learning Center *we do not hit or paddle children.* Hitting is often misunderstood by a young child, who does not always see the connection between a slap and some action on his part. Hitting as a form of punishment rarely stops an inappropriate behavior, but does cause confusion and anger.

At the Learning Center *we do not shout or yell at children.* Yelling usually frightens children and distracts them from the problem. Shouting, which is often accompanied by name calling on the part of the adult, also damages a child's self-esteem.

While the Learning Center staff respects the right of every parent to discipline his or her own child in a personal way (except where child abuse or neglect is concerned), parents who volunteer in the Center may not hit or shout at any child including their own. Hitting or shouting at a child in the presence of others upsets everyone and disturbs the classroom routine.

Acceptable Ways of Disciplining Children

The policies of the Learning Center regarding discipline do not mean that the staff wants to permit inappropriate behavior. Instead, the staff wishes to mold or change behavior using positive techniques. Some of these techniques include:

1. Developing with children rules that are stated at the children's developmental level.
2. Clarifying the consequences of disobeying rules before disobedience occurs; for example, "If you hit one of your friends you will not be allowed to play."

---

*Kathleen Pullan Watkins, "Learning Center Curriculum" (Philadelphia, PA: Philadelphia Parent-Child Center, 1988). Reprinted with permission.

Figure 1–7 SAMPLE DISCIPLINE POLICIES (continued)

3. Having age-appropriate expectations for children. We do not expect children to understand and obey complex rules.
4. Allowing children time to practice obeying new rules before punishing them for disobeying. Remember that toddlers have poorly developed memories and may not recall a new rule without a lot of practice.
5. Ignoring some kinds of inappropriate behavior. Some misbehavior is an attempt to get attention. The more attention the child gets, the more likely it is that the behavior will be repeated.
6. Giving a timeout for other types of inappropriate behavior. A timeout is another way of telling a child that his or her behavior is not acceptable. A timeout takes the child away from friends and activity for a short time, giving him or her a chance to start over or calm down.
7. Reinforcing desirable behavior by praising or rewarding the child. When the child realizes that attention comes from appropriate behavior, that behavior is more likely to continue.

Roles of Parents in the Discipline Process

Children are most likely to respond to attempts to discipline them when the adults involved are consistent; that is, when every adult who disciplines the child uses similar techniques.

Parents often find it difficult to be consistent at those times when family or financial pressures, or other stresses seem more important than a child's misbehavior. The parent may feel that keeping the child quiet, whatever it takes, is the only solution at that moment.

However, there are other solutions. One of the many roles of the Learning Center staff is to work together with parents to help children develop appropriate behaviors. Parents are invited and urged to discuss their concerns about their children's behavior with teachers and to plan together with staff means of responding consistently to problem behaviors. In this way, children will always get the same message from the important adults in their lives (parents and teachers) about those behaviors that are acceptable and those that are not.

Figure 1–8

SAMPLE ADMINISTRATIVE STRUCTURES

SAMPLE 1

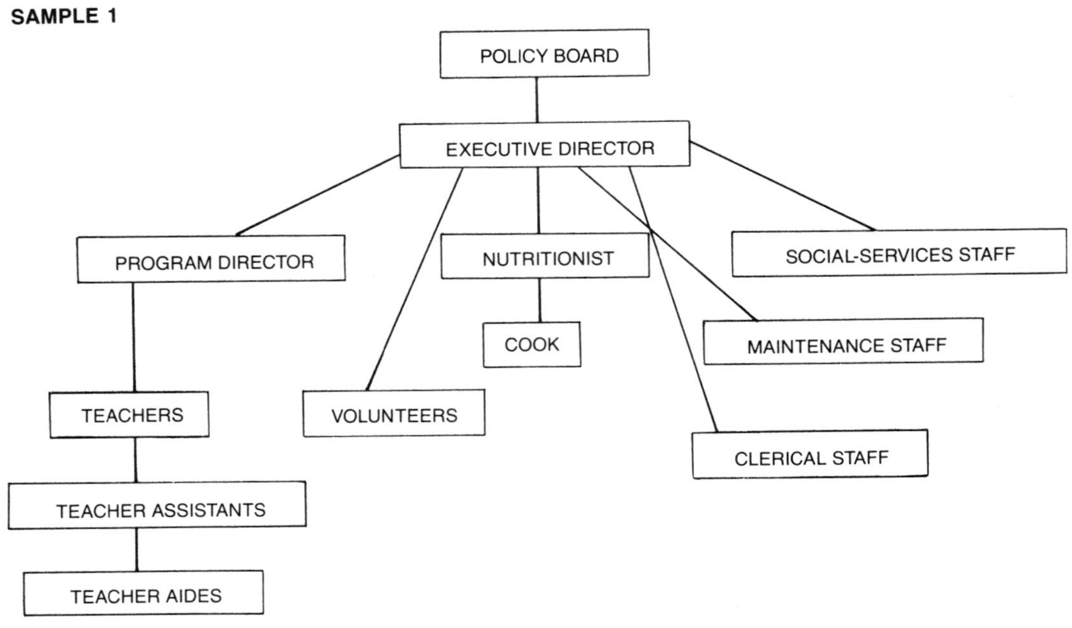

SAMPLE 2

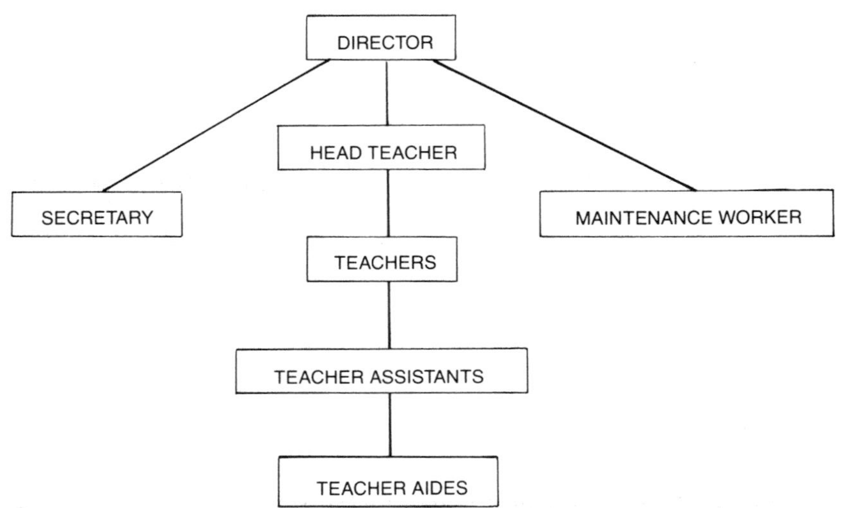

Figure 1–9

GUIDELINES FOR POLICY BOARD MEMBERS

1. Clarify the bylaws and roles to be played by the board.

2. Deal with issues that are the concern of the board. Leave classroom matters to the teaching staff, except under the most unusual circumstances, such as extremely inappropriate teacher behavior.

3. Respect the expertise of the early childhood staff.

4. Include representatives of groups who will be affected in discussions of new or different policies, like parents and staff.

5. Put new policies in writing and distribute them to staff and parents (where applicable).

6. Meet regularly on a designated schedule.

7. Ask staff and parents regularly for their input and concerns.

8. Evaluate the program director annually. Give feedback on performance and make suggestions for improvement.

Figure 1–10

GRANT CHILD DEVELOPMENT CENTER* BYLAWS

Article I. Name and Location
The corporate name of this body is the GRANT CHILD DEVELOPMENT CENTER, INC., whose administrative offices are located in Philadelphia, Philadelphia County, Pennsylvania.

Article II. Purpose
The purpose of this agency is the provision of child day care for children aged three to five years. Specifically, this agency provides a day-care and child-development program operating year around, Monday through Friday, during the hours 7:00 A.M. to 6:00 P.M.

Article III. Board of Directors
Section 1. The corporate powers of this body are vested in the Board of Directors, who shall control all matters of policy and expenditure of funds for the corporation.

Section 2. The Board of Directors shall consist of a minimum of four (4) and a maximum of six (6) members.

Section 3. The Board of Directors shall include the Center Director (as an ex officio member), one staff, and two parent representatives.

Section 4. Members of the Board of Directors shall be nominated and elected to office at the time of the annual meeting. It is the duty of elected members of the Board to attend the annual meeting and all such other meetings as shall be convened by the Board's Executive Officer. A Board member who misses two consecutive meetings will be replaced by the Board of Directors.

Section 5. The Board of Directors shall meet a minimum of once each year, with committee meetings scheduled as needed.

Section 6. A quorum for the transaction of any business shall be a majority of the number of Directors as stated in the articles of incorporation, and the act of the majority of the Directors present at a meeting at which a quorum (3) of the Directors is present shall be the act of the Board of Directors.

Article IV. Officers
Section 1. The Board of Directors shall elect annually from its numbers a president, vice-president, treasurer, and secretary. All Officers shall be elected for a term of two years.

---

*A fictional program.

Section 2. The President shall preside at all meetings and bear responsibility for the maintenance of corporate records, coordination of fund-raising efforts, and disbursement of funds.

Section 3. The Vice-president, in the absence of the President, shall preside and perform the President's duties.

Section 4. The Treasurer shall have the responsibility of keeping the Board informed of the Corporation's financial status. The Treasurer shall countersign checks in excess of an amount to be designated by the Board.

Section 5. The Secretary shall record and preserve the minutes of all the meetings of the Board of Directors and keep attendance records.

Article V. Standing Committees

Section 1. Fund-Raising Committee.
This committee shall:

1. Identify potential sources of income for the Grant Child Development Center.
2. Organize and carry out fund-raising events.

Section 2. Scholarship Committee.
This committee shall:

1. Review the names and qualifications of persons nominated for the Scholarship.
2. Update the Award Criteria at the request of the Board of Directors.

Section 3. Nominating Committee.
This committee shall:

1. Present a slate of officers at the annual meeting of the Board on alternate years. (Additional nominations may be made from the floor.)
2. Present names for election to the Board of Directors.
3. Present names to fill vacancies of offices as they occur.

Section 4. Curriculum Committee.
This commitee shall:

1. Review recommendations from staff and parents regarding curriculum innovations.
2. Review requests for special (large-purchase) equipment and materials used to implement the curriculum.

Section 5. Building and Grounds Committee.
This committee shall:

1. Review and approve plans for structural changes in the physical plant.
2. Raise funds for building projects.

Article VI. Amendments
These Bylaws may be amended at any regular meeting of the Board of Directors at which a quorum (3) of Directors is present by a two-thirds majority vote at such meeting. Notice of the general character of any proposed amendment must be provided to the membership at least ten (10) days prior to a Board meeting.

Further Reading

AXELROD, P. *Preschool and Child Care Administration*. Ann Arbor, MI: The University of Michigan, 1974.

BUTLER, A., et al. *Early Childhood Programs: Developmental Objectives and Their Use*. Columbus, OH: Merrill, 1975.

CLICK, P. *Administration of Schools for Young Children*. Albany, NY: Delmar Publishers, 1980.

DECKER, C., and J. DECKER. *Planning and Administering Early Childhood Programs*, 3rd ed. Columbus, OH: Merrill, 1984.

GROSSMAN, B.D., and C. Keyes. *Early Childhood Administration*. Boston: Allyn and Bacon, 1985.

HERBERT-JACKSON, E., et al. *The Infant Center: A Complex Guide to Organizing and Managing Infant Day Care*. Austin, TX: Pro-Ed, Inc., 1977.

HEWES, D., ed. *Administration: Making Programs Work for Children and Families*. Washington, DC: National Association for the Education of Young Children, 1979.

HILDEBRAND, V. *Management of Child Development Centers*. New York: Collier Macmillan Publishing, 1984.

MCMURPHY, J.R. *Day Care and Preschool Guide for Churches*. Chappaqua, NY: Christian Herald Books, 1981.

SCIARRA, D.J. and A. DORSEY. *Developing and Administering a Child Development Center*. Boston: Houghton Mifflin, 1979.

SEAVER, J.W. and C.A. CARTWRIGHT. *Child Care Administration*. Belmont, CA: Wadsworth Publishing Company, 1986.

SECOR, C.D. *Handbook for Day Care Board Members*, rev. ed. New York: Day Care Council of New York, 1984.

STEVENS, J.H. and E.W. KING. *Administering Early Childhood Education Programs*. Boston: Little, Brown and Company, 1976.

STRATA, D.F. *Administering Day Care and Preschool Programs*. Boston: Allyn and Bacon, 1982.

section 2

LICENSING, REGISTRATION, & ACCREDITATION OF DAY CARE & PRESCHOOL PROGRAMS

The management aids in this section focus on efforts to ensure proper and effective standards for facilities entrusted with the care and education of young children. They range from criteria for selecting a location for the facility to a sample directory of emergency services.

UNREGULATED FACILITIES

Across the United States there is a growing problem of unlicensed preschool and day care facilities. In the mistaken belief that anyone can provide for the needs of children, and sometimes with flagrant disregard for the applicable laws, day care centers, preschools, and nursery school programs are opening up daily in storefronts, homes, and church basements. True, there is a great demand for these services. Increasing numbers of families want or need child care and development programs for their young children. It is also true that parents often do not know a high-quality program from a poor one. Therefore, it becomes easy for parents to select a center or school on the basis of location, attractiveness of the physical plant, or charm of the director.

However, it is for the best of reasons that regulation of early childhood programs is required, including restrictions on who operates the program, where it is housed, and the type of learning environment it provides.

The reason that so many programs have been unable to go unregulated is simple. The monitoring agencies, usually branches of state offices, are often understaffed. Other factors are the lack of public education regarding quality programs, the fine distinction between some kinds of care (for example, family day care and babysitting), and parents' and the public's unwillingness to report unlicensed facilities.

METHODS OF MONITORING PROGRAMS

There are several ways for states to monitor early childhood facilities.

Licensing

Licensing is a highly structured process usually applicable to day care centers or other extended-day care facilities. It requires an applicant to meet rigid requirements regarding staff qualifications, physical plant, and child and staff health. There are even regulations governing the manner in which children may be transported by the center. To receive a license, a center must comply with all the regulations of the state in which the facility is located. Full compliance also requires the program to meet local health and safety ordinances.

This can be an expensive process. Few program directors have the luxury of beginning from scratch and designing a facility to meet local codes. Instead, major renovations must often be undertaken to get a certificate of occupancy for the building. Herein lies another reason for the growth of unregulated programs.

Figures 2–1 and 2–2 provide a checklist of factors to consider when choosing a site for a new program and a step-by-step procedure for obtaining a zoning variance. Figure 2–3 presents a detailed checklist covering items state licensing personnel are likely to review on a visit.

Registration

In recent years some states have adopted registration as a means to cope with the number of family day care homes. In one five-county region in Pennsylvania for example, there are close to 1,000 registered family day care homes. It would be impossible for the Commonwealth's Day Care Division to regularly visit each of these homes as there simply is not enough "people power." Registration has thus become a way of informing providers about the state's requirements for family day care homes, as well as a way of keeping track of where these facilities are and who operates them. It is not a completely satisfactory way of safeguarding the health and well-being of children attending, but it is far better than no regulation at all.

Figures 2–4, 2–5 and 2–6 show Commonwealth of Pennsylvania sample regulations for day care centers, group day care homes, and family day care homes.

State Licensure of Private Schools

Many nursery and preschool programs fall under the jurisdiction of the state's Department of Education, where they meet requirements similar to those set for private elementary schools. While some of these regulations are like those required of day care centers, others are less stringent. For example, the staff-child ratio is usually less in a school-length day or half-day program than that mandated for child day care where children are in attendance for periods of up to twelve hours.

State licensure covers health and safety, heating, lighting, credentials of the teaching and administrative staff, teaching loads, curriculum requirements, length of the school year, and other aspects of the program. Figure 2–7, "Sample Guidelines for Private Academic Schools," illustrates requirements in the areas of instruction, and health and welfare.

Some argue that requirements should be identical for two similar types of programs differentiated only by their primary aim—such as preschool education versus child day care. However, others believe that the two types of programs come under different jurisdictions and should thus be subject to different rules. Although this argument is sure to continue, some regulation is clearly better than none at all.

VOLUNTARY ACCREDITATION

Recently, there has been a new and revolutionary effort to support high-quality early childhood programs through voluntary accreditation. This is sponsored by the National Academy of Early Childhood Programs, a component of the National Association for the Education of Young Children, and entails a self-study component, a validation component, and finally an accreditation decision.*

If the staff and parents associated with a program feel they meet or would like to meet the Academy's Accreditation Criteria, they conduct a self-study. The self-study process makes it easy to identify areas where improvement in the program may be needed, to make changes, and to comply with the Academy's criteria. A description of how the program is in compliance with Academy criteria results from the self-study. Figure 2–8 "Sample Accreditation Criteria for Preschool and Nursery School Programs," presents some of the self-study criteria.

During the validation component, persons trained by the Academy visit the site of the program to determine the accuracy of the program description submitted by the agency. In the final stage, a committee established by the Academy determines whether accreditation will be awarded.

At present, the Academy's accreditation process is not widely known. Furthermore, while worthwhile, the self-study process is enormously timeconsuming and requires dedication on the part of the agency undertaking it. This may act as a deterrent to a less well organized or a new program.

---

*"Accreditation by the National Academy of Early Childhood Programs" (Washington, DC: National Association for the Education of Young Children).

REGULATING DAY CARE/PRESCHOOL PROGRAMS

It is the authors' contention that regulation of early childhood programs is more than important; it is crucial. These programs educate and care for children during the most vital and vulnerable period of their lives, a time when determination is made of how much of their potential will be fulfilled. Our society and children demand safe, well-managed programs that nurture and teach not only the young, but their parents as well.

The National Academy of Early Childhood Programs has made a valuable contribution to the early childhood profession and to the lives of families. Unfortunately, their efforts are not enough. Monitoring agencies at state and local levels must receive adequate funding in order to enforce existing regulations. Support must be garnered from legislators to effect changes in cases where regulations are substandard or nonexistent. Penalties must be enacted for persons who knowingly operate unlicensed, unregistered, or nonaccredited facilities. Lastly, the early childhood profession, together with others in the human services, and the federal government must undertake a campaign to educate the public. There must be an active unwillingness to accept poor-quality programs as a substitute for the high-quality ones children so richly deserve and so badly need.

GENERAL CHECKLISTS

The last two forms in Section 2 are general management tools that can be used with any program. Figure 2–9 "Building and Grounds Maintenance and Safety Checklist," covers virtually every physical area and situation in the preschool facility. Figure 2–10, "Sample Directory of Emergency Services for Health, Safety, and Family Assistance," provides a ready reference for obtaining help in all kinds of situations ranging from medical emergency and fire to locating a family counseling service or homeless shelter.

Figure 2–1

CRITERIA FOR PROGRAM SITE SELECTION

In those cases where an early childhood program is just being established and a site has not yet been selected, it is important for those identifying the site to consider many factors. The criteria listed below represent the ideal physical plant. It is highly unlikely that such a facility can be found, but one can be built. Whenever possible, efforts should be made to accommodate the needs of children, parents, and staff.

I. Classroom Criteria

- Ample open space indoors, at least 40 square feet per child who will participate in the program
- A number of windows for admission of natural light and ventilation, and use of outdoor scenery in classroom activities
- Smooth wood or linoleum floors that can easily be cleaned; old wall-to-wall carpeting can be bacteria-filled, difficult to clean, and expensive to remove
- Plentiful electrical outlets
- Storage space for supplies and equipment in or near the classroom
- All child-utilized facilities on the ground floor; fire escapes when classroom space must be above the first floor
- Easy access to the outdoors
- Uncluttered wall space for bulletin boards and displays of children's artwork

II. Restroom Criteria

- Restrooms near the classroom, with child-sized toilets and sinks; at least one toilet for every 15 children and one sink for every 25 children enrolled
- An area for a changing table and potty chairs when infants and toddlers are in care
- Storage space that can be locked for restroom supplies

III. Adult Space Criteria

- Space for an office, filing cabinets, and office machines
- Space for teachers to get away from the classroom, a lounge or rest area
- An adult bathroom
- A meeting place for parents and for parent-teacher conferences, with adequate space for adult seating

IV. Other Indoor Space Considerations

- A quite, separate space for isolating an ill or injured child
- Adequate space to store indoor and outdoor equipment (climbers, bicycles, balls, etc.)
- A kitchen with all appliances and storage space; important even if the program does not include meal service, since storage and preparation facilities may be important for food preparation activities done with the children

V. Outdoor Space Criteria

- Adequate play area, at least 65 square feet of accessible space
- Play area enclosed with durable, small-opening fencing material
- Smooth, grassy play area, free of open pits or animal-dug holes
- An area that is partially shaded during likely outdoor play times, such as from 10:00 A.M. to 12:00 P.M. and from 3:00 to 5:00 P.M.

Figure 2–2

SUGGESTIONS FOR OBTAINING A ZONING VARIANCE

Most municipalities and townships require that a permit be issued for the introduction of certain businesses into a locality. That is, each area is zoned for a specific use, such as residential or commercial. When a business owner or operator proposes a new use for that area he or she must apply for a permit. This permit is often referred to as a *zoning variance*.

Obtaining a variance for an area not already zoned for an early childhood program is often a very complex process. The legwork involved must be done by the business proprietor; in other words, if you do not do it, it will not get done. Here is a list of suggestions for obtaining a zoning variance when opening a day care center or preschool program.

Step 1: Visit your township or municipal services building. Take with you the exact address of the site or facility you wish to use. Telephoning is unwise because information can be misunderstood and a mistake could be extremely costly. Inquire about the type of zoning that would be required for your program and about the zoning already issued for the area where your site will be.

Step 2: If you will need to apply for a zoning variance, you will have to obtain a set of forms to be completed before your request can be reviewed. One of these will be a zoning application form, usually available at the township or municipal services building. The zoning board or town council will notify you regarding the scheduling of a public hearing to review your request.

You may also need to go to the local office of licenses and inspections where you can get a building permit if renovations must be made at an existing facility. If you are fortunate enough to be building a center, you will need to submit several sets of architect's plans to this office for approval. It is likely that some of the applications will cost money, fees for which vary greatly from one area to the next.

Step 3: The township or municipality will post a notice at your site describing the zoning change requested and giving the date of the public review hearing.

Figure 2–2 SUGGESTIONS FOR OBTAINING A ZONING VARIANCE (continued)

Step 4: Check with the businesses or homeowners in the area where you plan to open your facility. Ideally, of course, you should have done some feasibility studies before any other planning took place. Now, however, your check of public opinion must be an earnest one. Ask how people will feel about having a day care center next door or on their block. Find out if they have any special concerns or objections. If you are unable to respond to their questions at this time, be sure to have answers ready for the zoning hearing.

Step 5: The zoning board will meet, and you will be scheduled to appear before it to discuss your petition. All your applications, plans, and approvals must be in order at that time. Any failure to be prepared can cause a serious delay of the board's decision.

Bring evidence supporting the need for your program in the community and the support of neighbors, and be prepared to respond to any questions or challenges.

Step 6: If you have prepared thoroughly and no serious objections are raised by the community, you will be issued approval for a zoning variance enabling you to set up a facility at your site.

Please Note: The rules in your community may vary from these. Take time to check the applicable laws in your city or town. Remember, failure to obtain proper zoning can result in the closing of your program.

Figure 2–3

CHECKLIST FOR LICENSING OF DAY CARE CENTERS

The following represents a fairly inclusive list of the items that state child care licensing personnel would review during a visit for the purpose of granting a license or monitoring a previously licensed child day care facility. Be certain to check the specific licensing requirements in your state. This checklist applies to centers serving preschool age (three to five years) children.

I. Staffing Requirements

____ Staff meet all qualifications as indicated by personnel records
- Administrator/director
- Teachers
- Teacher assistants
- Teacher aides
- Food service worker/cook

____ Staff-child ratio is appropriate for the age of children and type of care or program provided*

II. Building and Physical Site

____ Building plans meet local safety and licensing requirements
____ Indoor space is adequate (at least 40 square feet per child)
____ Outdoor space is adequate (at least 65 square feet per child)
____ Outdoor hazards are barricaded or fenced off
____ Child care space is used only for that purpose
____ Children do not simultaneously nap and play in the same area
____ Toilets and sinks are adequate for the number of children served
____ Toilets and sinks are child-sized
____ Toilets are located nearby, but not in the classroom
____ Hot and cold running water is available
____ Water accessible to children does not exceed 110°F
____ All drugs, medicines, cleaners, poisons, and other toxic materials are stored out of children's reach
____ Painted surfaces are smooth and are neither chipped nor peeling
____ Paint used on premises contains no lead
____ There are no poisonous plants on the premises
____ Stairways have handrails and are properly lit

*Extended-day centers and infant-toddler programs generally require a higher staff-child ratio than do nursery schools and programs serving preschoolers.

____ Large glass surfaces (doors or picture windows) are marked for visibility

____ Facility has adequate ventilation

____ Windows accessible to children are screened or the amount they can be opened is limited to prevent children from falling out

____ Radiators and hot-water pipes are covered to prevent burns

____ Center has an operating telephone and listed telephone number

____ Exits are properly marked

III. Equipment

____ Equipment and materials are age-appropriate

____ Equipment and materials stimulate physical, cognitive, and psychosocial development

____ Equipment and materials used are free of any apparent hazards due to disrepair or safety problems

____ Outdoor equipment is safe and anchored in the ground

____ Swimming pools are fenced if left with standing water or are emptied after use

____ Individual bedding is provided for each child who naps while attending the program

____ Bedding is cleaned or washed weekly

IV. Children's Program

____ Program of daily activities is in writing

____ Daily activities promote development of the whole child

____ Staff refrains from corporal punishment

____ Efforts are made to identify children's special needs or handicapping conditions

____ Children are constantly supervised by staff

____ Children have regular outdoor activity

____ Children and staff wash hands regularly, especially before meals and after toileting

____ A parent or parent-authorized individual picks up and delivers the children to the center

V. Child Health

____ Age-appropriate health appraisals of all children are on file

____ Immunizations are up to date

_____ Health screening records are on file
_____ Emergency contact information is on file
_____ Emergency numbers (for police, fire, poison control) are on file
_____ A child isolation area is available in the event of illness
_____ Each classroom has a first-aid kit
_____ Pets kept on the grounds appear to be disease-free and well cared for

VI. Staff Health

_____ Staff health appraisals are on file and are up to date
_____ Written policies exist for the exclusion of a staff member with a communicable disease

VII. Food and Nutrition

_____ Meals and snacks are served to children in extended day programs
_____ Meals are balanced and nutritious
_____ Meals are served in age-appropriate portions
_____ Drinking water is available
_____ Drinking and eating utensils are safe and properly cleaned
_____ Proper food storage equipment is on premises

VIII. Transportation

_____ Center-owned vehicles are properly registered and insured
_____ Vehicle operators are properly licensed
_____ Vehicles contain first-aid kits
_____ Vehicle restraint systems (car seats or seat belts) are available for all children

Figure 2–4

SAMPLE REGULATIONS FOR DAY CARE CENTERS*

2–8A–71 STANDARDS.

2–8A–72 Staffing, Staff Responsibilities, and Staff Qualifications.

2–8A–73 The following staff qualifications shall be effective immediately with these exceptions:

- All staff currently employed in a day care center shall permanently qualify for their present position, as long as the staff qualifications in effect as of September 1, 1977 are met;
- Promotions prior to July 1, 1978, shall be permitted according to the staff qualifications in effect as of September 1, 1977, for director, group supervisor, assistant group supervisor, and aide. If promoted according to the staff qualifications in effect as of September 1, 1977, prior to July 1, 1978 these staff shall permanently qualify for their newly promoted positions.

All staff hired after April 2, 1978, and promoted after July 1, 1978, shall comply with the staff qualifications as specified in these regulations.

2–8A–74 The following staff titles are used in these regulations by the department for identification purposes only. As long as the staffing, staff responsibilities, and staff qualifications as specified in 2–8A–72 are met, the staff may be referred to by any title as designated by the provider or person directly administering the facility.

2–8A–75 All direct caregiving staff shall be at least seventeen years of age.

2–8A–76 All volunteers shall be at least fifteen years of age. Volunteers may be counted as direct caregiving staff in the staff-child ratio as long as the staff qualifications as specified in these regulations are met.

2–8A–77 An administrator shall be employed for each multitype day care system.

---

*Commonwealth of Pennsylvania, Department of Public Welfare, Office of Social Services, *Day Care Service for Children: Day Care Centers* (Harrisburg, PA: 1978).

2–8A–78 An administrator shall have the following responsibilities:

- Administering the operation of finances, personnel, maintenance, meal planning and preparation, janitorial services, and transportation, if provided
- Insuring that program objectives and activities are carried out
- Holding regular staff meetings to discuss program plans and interpret policies
- Providing for orientation and ongoing competency-oriented in-service training for all staff and volunteers
- Ensuring the maintenance of records and reports required by the department
- Assuring that the specific skills and training of the staff are reflective of the population served and,
- Designating a person to be responsible during the administrator's absence for any part of the day.

2–8A–79 An administrator shall have the following qualifications:

- Completion of a graduate program at an accredited college or university, with a master's degree in administration, early childhood education, child development, special education, elementary education, or the human-services field, at least fifteen credit hours in administration/supervision and/or child development related courses; *or*
- Completion of an undergraduate program at an accredited college or university, a bachelor's degree in administration, early childhood education, child development, special education, elementary education, or the human-services field and three years work experience in the human-services field which includes at least two in administration/supervison.

2–8A–80 A director shall be employed for each single-site day care center or multifacility day care system. Exception: Any single-site day care center providing care for 30 (or the closest higher multiple of the staff-child ratio of the children in care) or less children may employ a director/group supervisor who fulfills the responsibilities of both the director and the group supervisor and meets the qualifications of the director. The director/group supervisor may be included in direct caregiving staff for the period of the day when he or she is providing direct care for the children.

Figure 2–4 SAMPLE REGULATIONS FOR DAY CARE CENTERS (continued)

2–8A–81 When an administrator is not part of the staff, a director shall have the following responsibilities:

- Administering the operation of finances, personnel, maintenance, meal planning and preparation, janitorial services, and transportation if provided
- Insuring that program objectives and activities are carried out
- Holding regular staff meetings to discuss program plans and interpret policies
- Providing for orientation and ongoing competency-oriented in-service training for all staff and volunteers
- Insuring the maintenance of records and reports which are required by the department
- Assuring that the specific skills and training of the staff are reflective of the population served
- Designating a person to be responsible during the director's absence for any part of the day
- Supervising direct caregiving staff, *and*
- Developing the overall program.

2–8A–82 When an administrator is employed, a director shall have the following responsibilities:

- Coordinating and planning daily activities with the group supervisor
- Supervising direct caregiving staff
- Developing the overall program with the administrator
- Assisting the administrator in the administration of the facility.

2–8A–83 The director shall have the following qualifications:

- Completion of a graduate program at an accredited college or university with a master's degree in administration, early childhood education, child development, special education, elementary education, or the human services field; *or*
- Completion of an undergraduate program at an accredited college or university with a bachelor's degree in administration, early childhood education, child development, special education, elementary education, or the human-services field

and three years work experience in the human-services field, and two years work experience related to the care and development of children; *or*

- Completion of an undergraduate program at an accredited college or university with an associate's degree or its equivalent in administration, early childhood education, child development, special education, elementary education, or the human-services field, and four years work experience related to the care and development of children.

2–8A–84 A minimum of one group supervisor shall be employed for each facility providing care to any number of children. A ratio of one group supervisor to 45 (or the closest higher multiple of the staff-child ratio of the children in care) children shall be maintained for each facility providing care to more than 45 (or the closest higher multiple of the staff-child ratio of the children in care) children

2–8A–85 The group supervisor shall have the following responsibilities:

- Planning and implementation of daily program activities;
- Coordinating activities of assistant group supervisors and aides
- Assisting the director with designated activities

2–8A–86 A group supervisor shall have the following qualifications:

- Completion of an undergraduate program at an accredited college or university, a bachelor's degree in early childhood education, child development, special education, elementary education, or the human-services field; *or*
- Completion of an undergraduate program at an accredited college or university, an associate's degree and teaching certificate in early childhood education, child development, special education, elementary education, or the human-services field; *or*
- Completion of an undergraduate program at an accredited college or university, a bachelor's degree and teaching certificate in early childhood education, child development, special education, elementary education, or the human-services field and two years work experience related to the care and development of children.

2–8A–87 A minimum of one assistant group supervisor shall be employed for each facility providing care for any number of children. Additional assistant group supervisors shall be employed so that at least 50 percent of the direct caregiving staff is composed of persons with assistant group supervisor qualifications and responsibilities or above. Exception: For infants in similar developmental level groupings, a ratio of one assistant group supervisor to sixteen infants shall be maintained for each facility providing care to more than thirty-two infants.

2–8A–88 The assistant group supervisor shall have the following responsibilities:

- Assisting in the implementation of daily activities under the guidance of the group supervisor, *and*
- Coordinating daily activities and supervising aides in the absence of the group supervisor

2–8A–89 An assistant group supervisor shall have the following qualifications:

- A high-school diploma or general educational development certification; 15 credit hours in early childhood education, child development, special education, elementary education, or the human-services field; and one year work experience related to the care and development of children; *or*
- A high-school diploma or general educational development certification and three years work experience related to the care and development of children.

2–8A–90 Aides shall be employed, where needed, to maintain the staff-child ratios specified in 2–8A–97. No aide shall be left unsupervised at any time.

2–8A–91 The aide shall have the following responsibility:

- Assisting in the implementation of daily activities under the guidance of the group supervisor and/or the assistant group supervisor.

2–8A–92 An aide shall have the following qualifications:

- A high-school diploma or general educational development certification; *or*
- An 8th grade education and 2 years experience related to the care and development of children.

2–8A–97 Staff-Child Ratio.

2–8A–98 The following ratios of direct caregiving staff physically present with the children at any one time to children shall apply:

SIMILAR DEVELOPMENTAL LEVEL	*STAFF*	*CHILDREN*
Infants	1	4
Toddlers	1	5
Preschoolers	1	10
School-Age Children	1	12

MIXED DEVELOPMENTAL LEVEL	*STAFF*	*CHILDREN*
Infants/Toddlers	1	4
Infants/Toddlers/ Preschoolers/	1	6 (Including no more than 3 infants/ toddlers)
Infants/Toddlers/ Preschoolers/School-Age Children	1	6 (including no more than 3 infants/ toddlers)

MIXED DEVELOPMENTAL LEVEL	*STAFF*	*CHILDREN*
Infants/Toddlers/ School-Age Children	1	9 (including no more than 3 infants/ toddlers)
Preschoolers/School-Age Children	1	10 (including no more than 6 preschoolers)

2–8A–99 There shall be a minimum of 2 staff readily available at the facility at all times children are in care.

Figure 2–5

SAMPLE REGULATIONS FOR GROUP DAY CARE HOMES*

114. Child Health.

115. Each enrolled child shall have an age-appropriate health appraisal on record with the provider not more than 3 months following enrollment. Age-appropriate health appraisals shall be required and updated according to the recommended schedule for routine health supervision of the American Academy of Pediatrics. Health appraisals shall be certified by a licensed physician. The health appraisal shall include:

    - A review of previous health history
    - A physical examination
    - Growth assessments
    - A review and update of the child's immunization status to conform with the standards of the U.S. Public Health Service
    - Provision of age-appropriate screening tests according to the standards of the American Academy of Pediatrics
    - Any recommendations pertaining to medication required during the day, modifications or limitations of the child's activities and diet, and further medical tests or examinations that may be required
    - Development of a statement of the child's medical information pertinent to diagnosis and treatment in case of emergency
    - Development of a statement of recommendations for follow-up treatment or special care, if required.

116. A child who participates in the Department's Early and Periodic Screening Diagnosis and Treatment Program (EPSDT) is receiving a health service that meets the child health appraisal requirements as specified in 115. A record of the EPSDT screening instead of the child health appraisal as specified in 115 may be placed on the child's record.

117. Emergency contact information shall be easily accessible at all times that children are in the facility, being transported by the provider, and

---

* *Regulations for Group Day Care Homes* (Harrisburg, PA: Commonwealth of Pennsylvania, Department of Public Welfare Day Care Division, 1984).

on trips, including neighborhood excursions. This information shall be updated every six months and shall include:

- Name, address, and telephone number of the nearest hospital, police department, fire department, ambulance, and poison control center
- Means of transportation to the source of emergency care
- Name, address, and telephone number of the child's physician or source of medical care
- Any special medical information from the child's parent(s) or physician
- Any additional information on special needs of the child, specified by the child's parent(s) or physician, that might be helpful in handling an emergency situation.

118. Telephone numbers of the nearest hospital, police department, fire department, ambulance, and poison control center shall be posted by each telephone.

119. When emergency medical/surgical care is needed for a child, the parent(s) or the emergency contact person shall be notified as soon as practical for the best interests of the child. If the parents or emergency contact person cannot be reached, the caregiver shall record in writing the attempts made to inform the parents and emergency contact person.

120. The caregiver who accompanies a child to a source of emergency care shall remain with the child until parent(s) or designee assumes responsibility for the child's care.

121. No medication of any type, for example, cough drops, vitamins, aspirin, ear drops, Aspergum, or cough syrup, shall be given to a child without a physician's current (period of time specified on the instructions), written instructions and written consent from the child's parent(s).

122. A caregiver who accepts responsibility for administration of medication shall assure proper labeling of medication and record dose and times administered.

123. All medication in the facility shall be kept in a place inaccessible to children. All medications shall be kept in their original containers,

labeled with the original prescription label, and have safety-lock closures on the containers. All medication requiring refrigeration shall be refrigerated at the proper temperature.

124. Children shall not be separated from the group for illness unless separation provides for their own comfort or is required to provide adequate care for the group.

125. The day care staff shall have the option to deny care to ill children on any given day or to request that a child be removed from the facility if the child is determined by the day care staff to be too ill to remain in care. The parent(s) shall always be notified when a child becomes ill while in care. If the day care staff decides that a child is too ill to remain in the facility for the remaining period of the day, they shall notify the parent(s) immediately that the child must be picked up as soon as possible. If the day care staff decides that a child is too ill to be cared for on any given day, they shall notify the parent(s) upon receiving the child that care will not be provided. When a facility allows admission of ill children, a plan for care of such children shall be arranged with the parent(s) to assure that the needs of the child for rest, attention, and administration of prescribed medication, if applicable, are met. Contact with the parent(s) and the child's source of health care for purposes of consultation shall be readily available to the day care staff.

126. Each facility shall have a first-aid kit kept in a place inaccessible to children. The first-aid kit shall contain the following: soap, an assortment of adhesive bandages, sterile gauze pads, tweezers, tape, and scissors. The first-aid kit shall be taken on all trips, with the exception of neighborhood excursions.

127. At least one individual competent in first-aid techniques shall be present with the children whenever the children are in care. Competence shall be satisifed by successful completion of training provided by a public or private health professional.

128. Any pet or animal present at the facility, indoors or outdoors, shall be in good health, show no evidence of carrying disease, and be a friendly companion for the children. This shall also apply to those pets or animals present at the facility that do not belong to the caregiver or the caregiver's family.

129. Staff Health.

130. Each caregiver, volunteers who serve on a regular basis, and family members providing direct care for the children on a regular basis shall have a health appraisal within three months prior to providing initial day care service and annually thereafter. Health appraisals shall be certified by a licensed physician. The health appraisal shall include:

- A physical examination
- Tuberculosis screening and follow-up that assures freedom from communicable TB (screening required only every two years)
- Detection of any chronic diseases that require medication or restriction of activity
- Any information noting any special medical problems that would interfere with the health of the children or prohibit the caregiver from providing adequate care for the children

If day care service to children is interrupted or is sporadic during the year, one annual health appraisal shall be sufficient, as long as the health appraisal is performed three months prior to providing initial day care service.

131. Caregivers with cold sores (herpes) infections shall not be permitted to care for infants under three months of age.

Figure 2–6

SAMPLE REGULATIONS FOR FAMILY DAY CARE HOMES*

39. Building and Physical Site.

40. All floors, walls, ceilings, and other surfaces, including the outdoor play area, must be kept clean and in good repair.

41. All medicines, drugs, cleaning materials, detergents, aerosol cans, and other poisonous and toxic materials must be stored in their original, labeled containers and used in such a way that does not contaminate play surfaces, food, food preparation areas or constitute a hazard to the children. Such materials must be kept in a place inaccessible to children and separate from child care areas, food, and food preparation areas.

42. Fixed and portable space heaters and wood-burning stoves are permitted to be used while children are in care, only if inspected and approved in writing by the State Department of Labor and Industry, a local fire marshall, a local fire department (volunteer or professional), or other local fire safety agency. A copy of this written approval must be kept on file.

43. Hot water pipes, fixed and portable space heaters, wood-burning stoves, and other sources of heat exceeding 110° F (43° C) which are accessible to children must be equipped with protective guards or insulated to prevent children from coming in direct contact with the heat source. Fireplaces must be securely screened or equipped with protective guards while in use.

44. The family day care home must have one indoor flush toilet and one sink with water available at the sink.

45. All windows and doors used for ventilation must be screened.

46. The family day care home must have a working telephone.

47. Stairways, hallways, and exits from rooms and from the family day care home must be unobstructed. Easily opened protective gates and other devices are permitted.

**Regulations for Family Day Care Homes* (Harrisburg, PA: Commonwealth of Pennsylvania, Department of Public Welfare, Bureau of Program Development and Implementation, 1986).

48. Protective receptacle covers must be placed in all electrical outlets accessible to children under five years of age.

49. An operable smoke detector must be placed on each level of the home used by the children and on each level of exit from the home.

50. A portable fire extinguisher suitable for Class B fires must be provided in the kitchen and other cooking areas. The fire extinguisher must be tested yearly or have a gauge to assure adequate pressure level.

51. Equipment.

52. Play equipment and materials must be provided that are appropriate to the development needs, individual interests, and ages of the children. There must be a sufficient amount of play equipment and material so that there is not excessive competition and long waits.

53. Toys, play equipment, and other indoor and outdoor equipment used by the children must be kept clean, in good repair, and free from rough edges, sharp corners, pinch and crush points, splinters, and exposed bolts. All ladders on slides must have guards along the sides.

54. Outdoor equipment, such as climbing apparatus, slides, and swings, must be anchored firmly and be in good repair. Outdoor equipment at the family day care home must not be located on either concrete or asphalt surfaces.

55. Toys and objects with a diameter of less than 1 inch (2.5 centimeters), objects with removable parts having a diameter of less than 1 inch (2.5 centimeters), plastic bags, and styrofoam objects must not be accessible to children who are still placing objects in their mouths.

56. The following materials must be available in the family day care home: soap, sterile gauze pads, tweezers, tape, and scissors.

57. Each child, except school-age who do not take naps, must have clean, age-appropriate rest equipment.

58. If night care is provided (children are sleeping at the family day care home), each child must have a bed equipped with comfortable springs, mattress, sheets, pillow, pillowcase, and blankets. No children shall share a single bed.

Figure 2–6 SAMPLE REGULATIONS FOR FAMILY DAY CARE HOMES (continued)

59. All children must be directly supervised (caregiver physically present with the children) at all times children are wading or swimming.

60. Above-ground and in-ground swimming pools must be made inaccessible to children, when children are not swimming.

61. Portable wading pools must be emptied and cleaned daily.

Figure 2–7

SAMPLE GUIDELINES FOR PRIVATE ACADEMIC SCHOOLS*

PROGRAM OF INSTRUCTION

55.31 Curriculum.

A. The following subjects shall be taught in the English language and from English texts:

1. English, including listening, spelling, reading, speaking, and writing

2. Arithmetic

3. Geography

4. History of the United States and this Commonwealth.

5. Civics, including loyalty to the governments of this Commonwealth and the United States

6. Safety education

7. Humane treatment of birds and animals

8. Health, including physical education and physiology

9. Music and art

B. Cruel experiments on any living animal shall not be permitted.

Cross Reference

This section cited in 22 Pa. Code Section 59.21 (relating to program of instruction).

**Rules and Regulations Governing Private Academic Schools* (Harrisburg, PA: Commonwealth of Pennsylvania, Department of Education, 1987).

55.32 Constitution of the United States.

There shall be regular courses of instruction in the Constitution of the United States beginning not later than the opening of the eighth grade.

Cross Reference

This section cited in 22 Pa. Code Section 59.21 (relating to program of instruction).

HEALTH AND WELFARE

55.41 Isolation of students with contagious infections.

Schools shall meet the requirements of Section 53.42 of this Title (relating to isolation of students with contagious infections).

Figure 2–8

SAMPLE ACCREDITATION CRITERIA FOR PRESCHOOL AND NURSERY SCHOOL PROGRAMS*

The voluntary accreditation process developed by the National Academy of Early Childhood Programs consists of three components. The first of these is a self-study mechanism that enables a program to be intensively evaluated from within by the director, staff, and parents. The self-study provides avenues for recognizing the need for and effecting changes that influence in a positive way the quality of the program. Following is an outline of some of the self-study criteria. Note that each of the sections listed has extensive subcriteria to be met by a program. Further information on the Academy's accreditation process may be obtained by writing or calling:

National Academy of Early Childhood Programs
National Association for the Education
 of Young Children
1834 Connecticut Avenue N.W.
Washington, D.C. 20009
202-232-8777/800-424-2460

I. Observation in the Early Childhood Classroom

- **A.** Staff-child interactions
- **B.** Curriculum
- **C.** Classroom environment
- **D.** Safety and health of children and staff
- **E.** Nutrition and food service

II. Report of the Program Administrator

- **A.** Curriculum
- **B.** Interactions between staff and parents
- **C.** Staff qualifications and staff development component
- **D.** Administrative functioning
- **E.** Staffing
- **F.** Physical environment

**Guide to Accreditation* (Washington, DC: National Academy of Early Childhood Programs, a division of NAEYC, 1985).

Figure 2–8 ACCREDITATION CRITERIA—PRESCHOOL/NURSERY (continued)

G. Program health and safety status
H. Nutrition and food service
I. Evaluations conducted by the program

III. Questionnaire for Staff

A. Interactions between staff and parents
B. Staff qualifications and staff development
C. Program administration
D. Staffing
E. Health and safety of children and staff
F. Evaluations of staff by administration

IV. Questionnaire for Parents (examples of questions only)

A. Do parents receive information about program philosophy and goals for children?
B. Do parents receive information about meal and snack menus?
C. Do parents and teachers talk about important aspects of childrearing, like feeding and discipline?
D. Do parents always feel welcome at the center?
E. Do parents regularly get information on day-to-day center activities?
F. Are parents regularly asked to evaluate the program?
G. Are parents satisfied with the care and education provided for their child by the program?

Figure 2–9

BUILDING AND GROUNDS MAINTENANCE AND SAFETY CHECKLIST

Area 1: Offices

____ Typewriters and office machines serviced
____ Supplies inventoried and ordered as needed
____ Carpeting clean and tacked down
____ Telephone in operation
____ Emergency numbers available and current

Area 2: Bathrooms

____ Water temperature appropriate (110°F or less)
____ Toilets and sinks in working order, no leaks
____ Paper and soap supplies adequate
____ Windows secure and barred (where appropriate)
____ Medicines, cleaners properly stored
____ Diapers properly disposed of

Area 3: Classrooms

____ Consumable supplies inventoried and ordered as needed
____ Carpeting clean and tacked down
____ Windows secure and barred (where appropriate)
____ Radiators covered
____ Outlets covered
____ Fire extinguisher available and serviced
____ First-aid kit available and with adequate supplies
____ Toys and equipment checked for damage and injury-causing pieces
____ Electric cords are out of reach, not dangling

Figure 2–9 BUILDING AND GROUNDS CHECKLIST (continued)

____ Heavy equipment not stored where it will fall and injure children
____ Equipment not blocking exits
____ Exits clearly marked
____ Fire escape procedures posted
____ Wooden floors smooth, clean, and without splinters
____ Poisonous plants removed
____ Emergency numbers available and current

Area 4: Kitchen

____ Water temperature appropriate for dishwashing
____ Fire extinguisher available and serviced
____ Cleaners and insecticides properly stored away from food
____ Refrigerator and freezer are proper temperature
____ Gas stove turns off completely, no gas leaks or odor of gas
____ First-aid kit available and with adequate supplies

Area 5: Play Yard

____ Yard fenced or otherwise cut off from street traffic areas
____ Trash stored away from play area
____ Equipment checked for damage or injury-causing pieces and serviced regularly
____ Grass cut regularly
____ Sand box checked for stones and glass
____ Holes or open areas accessible to children are covered or closed off
____ Poisonous plants and shrubs removed

Other Concerns

____ Peeling or chipped paint
____ Uncovered hot-water or heating pipes
____ Uncovered trash receptacles
____ Swimming or wading pools left full

Figure 2–10

SAMPLE DIRECTORY OF EMERGENCY SERVICES FOR HEALTH, SAFETY, AND FAMILY ASSISTANCE

AGENCY	*ADDRESS (WHERE APPROPRIATE)*	*TELEPHONE (ENTER LOCAL NUMBER)*
Fire/Medical Emergency		
Police		
Poison Control		
Child Abuse/Neglect Hotline		
Abused Women/Shelter		
AIDS Information/Counseling		
Alcohol Abuse		
Clothing Assistance		
Crisis Intervention		
Drug Abuse		
Family Counseling		
Food Assistance		
Handicapped Services:		
Hearing/Speech		
Mental Retardation		
Orthopedic Impairment		
Vision		
Homeless Shelter		

Figure 2–10 SAMPLE DIRECTORY OF EMERGENCY SERVICES (continued)

Hospital ____________________

Housing Assistance ____________________

Pregnancy Problems ____________________

Public School (local) ____________________

Parochial School (local) ____________________

Runaways
(national and local switchboards) ____________________

Senior Services ____________________

Suicide Prevention ____________________

Venereal Disease ____________________

Veterans' Services ____________________

Further Reading

Administration of Child Care Programs: Business Management. Lubbock, TX: Home Economics Curriculum Center, Texas Tech University, 1983.

BREITHBART, V. *The Day Care Book: The Why, What, and Home of Community Day Care*. New York: Knopf, 1977.

CARTER, MARGIE, "NAEYC Center Accreditation Project: What's It Like in Real Life?" *Child Care Information Exchange*, May 1986, pp. 38–41.

COLLINS, R.C., "Child Care and the States: The Comparative Licensing Study," *Young Children*, 38(5), July 1983, pp. 3–11.

Comparative Licensing Study: Profiles of State Day Care Licensing Requirements. Washington, DC: Laurence Johnson Associates, 1981–1982.

Early Childhood Directors Association of St. Paul, MN. *Survival Kit for Directors*. St. Paul, MN: Toys 'n Things Press, 1984.

"How to Start a Child Care Center." *Report on Preschool Programs*. Special Report, June 11, 1986.

KAHN, A., and S. KAMERMAN. *Child Care: Facing the Hard Choices*. St. Paul, MN: Toys 'n Things Press, 1988.

KENDALL, E.D., and L.H. WALKER. "Day Care Licensing: The Eroding Regulations." *Child Care Quarterly*, 13 (4), Winter 1984, pp. 278–89.

LEHRMAN, K. and J. PACE. *Day Care Regulation: Serving Children or Bureaucrats?* Cato Institute Policy Analysis No. 59, Washington, DC: Cato Institute, September 1985.

National Academy of Early Childhood Programs. *Guide to Accreditation*. Washington, DC: National Association for the Education of Young Children, 1985.

Policy Issues in Day Care: Summaries of 21 Papers. Washington, DC: U.S. Department of Health, Education and Welfare, 1977.

ZIGLER, E.F., and E.W. GORDON (Eds.) *Day Care: Scientific and Social Policy Issues*. Boston: Auburn House, 1982.

section 3

FISCAL MANAGEMENT OF EARLY CHILDHOOD PROGRAMS

Financial management is a key administrative responsibility. The forms in this section will help you develop the necessary record-keeping tools and seek out extra funding from sources such as foundations and via the planning of special fund-raisers.

PROGRAM PLANNING

Program planning must include a realistic appraisal of the resources—human, physical, and financial—that are important for the operation of the program. These factors play a vital role when center goals, both short- and long-term, are being planned by directors and boards of directors. Identifying specific financial duties and the staff members responsible for them are important administrative functions.

In most cases, a written program plan accompanied by a budget covering the areas shown in Figure 3–1, "Sample Budget Format," is submitted yearly. Funding agencies generally require evidence of sound financial management, for which purposes detailed, written specifics of a center's financial administration and health may be requested. These written specifics may also be used for answering parents' questions concerning center finances.

RECORD KEEPING/ACCOUNTING

A sound, properly maintained record-keeping/accounting system is an important tool for reflecting the fiscal health of the program. All financial transactions must be recorded. Tax forms based on the types of records identified in Figure 3–2, "Records Criteria for Tax Purposes," must be completed and filed at the required times. The penalties for late filing may be costly to a center.

To ensure easy maintenance in the event a substitute or new bookkeeper must take over, a standardized format should be used for record keeping. It is important that an independent audit be conducted annually by a reputable accountant (preferably a CPA). Internal controls must also be fashioned, including procedures and forms to guard against unauthorized use of funds. Finally, a variety of records should be maintained for such items as:

Personnel

Employee time and attendance

Employee leave time (vacation, compensatory, sick, overtime)

Individual employee earnings

Fringe benefits

Supplies and equipment

Consumables (instructional, food services, medical, maintenance, and office)

Inventories

Attendance (children)

Tuition

Board resolutions/ committee actions

Travel reimbursement

Receipt form for fees

In-kind contributions/local share (may be required by federally funded programs)

Grants

Service Contributions (volunteers' time/donated goods)

Cash contributions

Contracted services

Property rental

Minutes of board and staff meetings

Insurance forms

Inspections

Figure 3–3, "Sample Parent's Contract for Services," provides two sample contracts for preschool services, the first specifying a weekly fee payment and the second a monthly payment. Figures 3–4 and 3–5 present two related forms, "Sample Fee Collection Notice" and "Sample Receipt for Fees Collected."

Fiscal procedures include obtaining a federal identification number through your local Internal Revenue office. This number if necessary for obtaining tax-exempt status. It is also important to secure a state unemployment insurance identification number, which must appear on state-required reports of wages paid and employee termination notices.

Simplified recording systems can be used to list income and expenditures. Regardless of the system used, it must provide accurate information on all transactions. Entries should be made whenever a transaction takes place and the transactions should be totaled monthly.

SPECIAL FUNDING SOURCES

Many preschool programs must rely on sources other than fees for funds necessary to make major improvements in the facility and instructional programs. Six different forms for special fundraising activities are provided here. Figure 3–6 presents criteria for applying for a grant, outlining the elements usually required when applying for a foundation grant. This is followed by a proposal submission checklist (Figure 3–7) to help you ensure that all necessary steps have been taken in the preparation of a grant proposal. Next is a complete minigrant proposal (Figure 3–8). Other forms include a sample fund-raising letter (Figure 3–9) for a building project, examples of fundraising activities (Figure 3–10), and a sample thank-you letter for donated services (Figure 3–11).

EVALUATION

The evaluative process is the last but an equally important step in the fiscal management process. A program's effectiveness is measured against service goals and its budget handling. Realistic planning and the maintenance of functional procedures provide the basis for a smooth and orderly evaluation. Evaluation of the fiscal management component should reveal (1) whether personnel records have been kept accurately and to the satisfaction of the auditors; (2) whether payments have been made to vendors in a timely fashion; (3) whether the financial records provide the director with current information, enabling him or her to assess the need for necessary fiscal changes; and (4) under careful and close examination and with program and fiscal management evaluation reviewed jointly, whether program goals were met; and on competitive cost-effective basis, whether the amount of resources spent were justified.

Fiscal management excellence necessitates that a coherent set of managerial procedures be instituted and vigilant compliance be enforced to ensure a healthy financial base for the program.

Figure 3–1

SAMPLE BUDGET FORMAT

A. Personnel

1. Full-Time Personnel

	NO. OF STAFF	POSITION TITLE	× PERCENT OF TIME	× NO. OF MOS.	ITEM'S COST
1.	______	______	______	______	______
2.	______	______	______	______	______
3.	______	______	______	______	______
4.	______	______	______	______	______
5.	______	______	______	______	______
6.	______	______	______	______	______
7.	______	______	______	______	______

Subtotal Full-Time Personnel: ______

2. Part-Time Personnel

	NO. OF STAFF	POSITION TITLE	BASIS FOR COST ESTIMATE (RATE/DAY × NO. OF DAYS)		
1.	______	______	______	______	______
2.	______	______	______	______	______
3.	______	______	______	______	______
4.	______	______	______	______	______

Subtotal Part-Time Personnel: ______

Subtotal All Personnel: ______

Figure 3–1 SAMPLE BUDGET FORMAT (continued)

3. **Fringe Benefits**
(FICA, SUI, Workman's Compensation, health insurance, disability, retirement, etc.) ________

Subtotal Fringe Benefits: ________

4. **Consultants and Contract Services**

NATURE OF SERVICE	*BASIS FOR COST* (*RATE/DAY × NO. OF DAYS*)	
		________

Subtotal Consultants and Contract Services: ________

Total Personnel: ________

B. Nonpersonnel

1. **Supplies and Services** ________
Consumable supplies (maintenance, office, classroom) ________
Printing ________
Copying ________
Telephone ________
Mail ________
Insurance ________
Subscription ________
Computer cost ________

Subtotal Supplies and Services: ________

2. **Equipment** ________
Purchase ________
Lease ________

Subtotal Equipment: ________

Figure 3–1 SAMPLE BUDGET FORMAT (continued)

3. **Travel**
   Local ________
   Out-of-town ________
   ____

Subtotal Travel: ________

4. **Space**
   Rent ________
   Maintenance ________
   Utilities ________
   ____

Subtotal Space: ________

Total Nonpersonnel: ________

C. Total Direct Cost (A + B) ________

D. Total Indirect Cost ________

E. Total Costs (C + D) ________

Figure 3–2

RECORDS CRITERIA FOR TAX PURPOSES

The following are examples of the types of records that should be kept for tax purposes:

Income

Gross receipts
Gross profits
Other income

Deductions

Advertising
Bad debts, i.e., unpaid fees for services
Bank service charges
Car/van/truck expenses (repairs, insurance, maintenance, mileage, name of user, business reasons for trips)
Employee benefits programs
Insurance
Laundry and cleaning
Legal and professional services
Office expenses
Pension plans
Rent on business property
Taxes
Supplies and materials (used for educational purposes)
Utilities
Telephone
Dues for professional organizations and subscriptions to business magazines and journals
Postage and shipping
Printing and reproduction
Business licenses and fees
Expendables (food and materials that will be expendable within the year)
Depreciable property (deductions are spread out over the useful life of property, for example, cars, carpets, furniture, playground equipment, washer-dryer)

Note: Keep a separate checking account for day care business.

Figure 3–3A

SAMPLE PARENT'S CONTRACT FOR SERVICES

SAMPLE 1: WEEKLY FEE PAYMENT

This is a contract between ______________________ (Name of Parent) and ______________________ (Name of Provider) for the day care of ______________________ (Name of Child) for five days per week, Monday through Friday. ______________________ (Name of Child) will not be brought to the center before 7 A.M. and will not be picked up later than 6 P.M. The fee will be $__________ per week, payable on Monday of each week. If ______________________ (Name of Child) is absent one day, the fee is the same. If the child is absent more than two days in a week due to illness or family emergency, ______________________ (Name of Parent) will not have to pay for services on those days. If the child is absent from care for nonmedical reasons for two or more days without prior notification to the center by the parent, that parent shall be responsible for fees for services on the days of absence. ______________________ (Name of Parent) will provide proof of a complete medical checkup and current immunizations. After ______________________ (Name of Child) has been absent due to illness, ______________________ (Name of Parent) will provide ______________________ (Name of Provider) with a release from a medical authority before child can return to day care services. ______________________ (Name of Parent) will pay $__________ per hour overtime when ______________________ (Name of Child) is not picked up by 6 P.M.

Signature of Parent ______________________ Date __________

Signature of Director or Designee ______________________

Date __________

Figure 3–3B

SAMPLE 2: MONTHLY FEE PAYMENT

Date ____________

____________________ will be attending the ____________________ for
(Name of Child) (Name of Provider)

day care services beginning ____________________, from 7 A.M. to 6 P.M. for
(Date)

a monthly fee of $__________ payable in full in advance at the beginning of each month. ____________________ will attend five days per week. If
(Name of Child)

____________________ is absent for more than three consecutive days
(Name of Child)

due to personal illness, fees for that period will be suspended. ____________________ will provide ____________________ with a release
(Name of Parent) (Name of Provider)

from a licensed medical authority before child can return to day care services. $__________ per hour overtime is charged when child arrives before 7 A.M. or is picked up after 6 P.M. All necessary immunizations are required before child can begin attending ____________________.
(Name of Provider)

____
(Date)

____
(Parent's Signature)

____
(Director/Administrator's Signature)

Figure 3–4

SAMPLE FEE COLLECTION NOTICE

____
(Name of Provider)

Account Number ________________ Date ____________

____
(Name of Parent)

____
(Address of Parent)

Total Amount Due
$ ______________

It is urgent that you contact ____________________ (Name of Contact Person) immediately upon receipt of this letter to discuss your reasons for nonpayment of child day care services for ____________________ (Name of Child) as agreed to in your contract. We feel that it is important for services to your child to continue without unnecessary and unwarranted interruptions. To avoid suspension of services and to resolve your account please call or come by the center as soon as possible. If we do not hear from you by __________ (Date) at __________ (Time), we will assume that you no longer desire day services for ____________________ (Name of Child).

The amount of $__________ outstanding still requires payment, and a deduction shall be applied against your first month's advance tuition payment.

Sincerely,

____
(Name of Director)

Figure 3–5

SAMPLE RECEIPT FOR FEES COLLECTED

Statement for period ending ____________ for day care services received from

	Account No.	Amount Due
______________________________ (Name or Provider)	____________	$00.00
______________________________ (Address of Provider)		Amount Paid
______________________________ (Telephone No. of Provider)		$__________

Due upon enrollment:

Fee for first month's tuition $__________

Deposit equal to one month's tuition $__________
(Will be applied to last month's tuition, providing one month's notice of withdrawal from program is given.)

____
(Name of Parent)

____
(Name of Child)

____
(Address of Parent)

PAYMENTS ARE DUE AND PAYABLE ON THE FIRST OF THE MONTH

Figure 3–6

CRITERIA FOR GRANT APPLICATION

1. *Cover Letter.* Affords you the opportunity to present the features of your proposal most likely to be of interest to the foundation or funding source.
2. *Table of Contents.* Organizes the presentation and outlines the information contained. It offers a preview of the facts and figures in your proposal.
3. *Summary of the Proposal.* Describes the specific purpose of the grant, and introduces your organization, the minimum amount of money requested, and the projected outcomes of the proposal.
4. *Qualifications.* Prepare documented evidence of your staff's achievements using supporting evidence from organizations familiar with your work and that have endorsed your agency's abilities. Include information on staff members and professionals who will serve as consultants to the project. A summary of relevant data is important for this section.
5. *Problem Statement.* Allows the chance to focus on the specific needs to be met and identification of the population group(s) to be served by the project.
6. *Goals and Objectives.* Describes the specific objectives whose attainment will provide concrete measurement for meeting your goals. The goal of your project is the ultimate accomplishment the program can achieve.
7. *Methods.* Describes how objectives will be achieved. Also specify a timetable for each phase of the project, including commencement and termination dates for a grant.
8. *Evaluation.* Criteria used to analyze how well you have accomplished the project's goals and objectives.
9. *Budget.* Provide specific details on how you plan to spend the requested funds.
10. *Future Funding.* Describes your plans for financing the project at the termination of the grant. Grantors need to be assured of project's continued survival once funded.
11. *Appendix.* Include supportive documents, for example, letters of endorsement, validity of tax-exempt status, resumes of staff, publications by or about your organization, publicity.

Figure 3–7

PROPOSAL SUBMISSION CHECKLIST

____ **1.** Have you identified foundations with an established interest in projects like yours?

____ **2.** Have you sent propspective foundations a preliminary letter outlining a need for the project and soliciting their interest in receiving a full proposal?

____ **3.** Have you made contact with the staff of prospective foundations to establish a positive future relationship?

____ **4.** Does your organization have nonprofit status?

____ **5.** Did you prepare an original cover letter designed for each prospective grantor?

____ **6.** Have you adhered to all necessary application deadlines?

____ **7.** Is your proposal of reasonable length (usually under ten pages)?

____ **8.** Does your proposal show:

- ____ **a.** Audited financial statement for your organization
- ____ **b.** Projected budget
- ____ **c.** One-page summary of your proposal
- ____ **d.** Statement of problem
- ____ **e.** Description of goals and objectives
- ____ **f.** Description of methodology
- ____ **g.** Staff qualifications
- ____ **h.** Criteria for evaluation
- ____ **i.** Future funding plans

____ **9.** Has your proposal been reviewed by person(s) knowledgeable and successful in securing grants?

____ **10.** Has your budget been reviewed to refine your expense estimates?

Figure 3–8

SAMPLE MINIGRANT PROPOSAL*

INTRODUCTION

The congregation of First Episcopal Church of Germantown, Pennsylvania, proposes to develop and operate a pilot day care program for twelve children, ages three to five years. The day care program is to be situated at 213 Valley Drive, Germantown, on property owned by/adjacent to First Episcopal Church, this site having been previously approved and zoned for a child care facility by the Children's Services Division of the Pennsylvania Department of Public Welfare and the Zoning Board of the City of Germantown, respectively.† Appropriate licensing for the day care center will be awarded by the Children's Services Division at such time when building renovations at 213 Valley Drive permit conformity with day care regulations of the Commonwealth of Pennsylvania.

The congregation of First Episcopal Church supports the development of a day care program, approving the program by a vote of church membership on May 18, 1980.

THE NEED FOR CHILD CARE

Past surveys of the congregation of First Episcopal Church have revealed a significant need among families in its membership for child care services. Furthermore, cutbacks in funding of federally funded programs, effective in the 1988–89 fiscal year, will place severe limitations on the number of slots available for children in the Germantown community. The proposed facility will, therefore, serve the needs of the Church congregation, as well as the needs of nonmember families in the surrounding neighborhood.

PROGRAM PURPOSE AND PHILOSOPHY

The day care center of First Episcopal Church will be designed in order to meet the growing need of its congregation and of the Germantown community for child day care services. The day care center will further serve to build new links and strengthen previously established ones with the surrounding community. This will be accomplished via the exploration and use of local resources that will serve to improve and maximize the quality of the child care program.

The day care center is to be established and the program implemented

---

* *Regulations for Child Day Care Centers.* (Harrisburg, PA: Bureau of Child Development Programs, Department of Public Welfare, Publication #C1-201, 1981).

† See attachments

based on the concepts that quality child care improves and strengthens family relationships by providing a safe and nurturing environment for the child, enabling the parent(s) to be employed or pursue other work necessary for the support and well-being of the family, and that day care programs should be geared toward fostering the physical, social-emotional, and cognitive development of the whole child.

GOALS FOR THE PROGRAM*

1. To provide day care services for the children, ages three to five, of the First Episcopal Church congregation.
2. To provide day care services for the children, ages three to five, of families in the Germantown community.
3. To provide a day care program that includes educational, social-services, health/nutrition, and parent/community involvement components.
4. To develop new links and maintain and extend existing ones between First Episcopal Church and the Germantown community.

OBJECTIVES OF THE PROGRAM*

1. The program will provide child care services for twelve preschool age children (3 to 5 years), five days per week, during the hours from 7 A.M. until 6 P.M.
2. Children attending the day care program will participate on a daily basis in outdoor and indoor activities designed to foster the development of large and small muscles.
3. Children attending the day care program will receive daily mid-morning and midafternoon snacks provided in accordance with their age and nutritional needs.
4. Qualified residents of the Germantown community will be considered for the teaching and volunteer positions among the day care center staff.

ELIGIBILITY FOR DAY CARE SERVICES

Children aged three to five years will be recruited from among the families comprising the congregation of First Episcopal Church, as well as from families living in the Germantown community, and children will be accepted into the day care program on a first-come, first-served basis.

Fees for day care services will be charged on a sliding-scale basis accord-

*Additional goals and objectives will be developed for various program components.

ing to family income. This fee scale will be determined by the Advisory Board of the day care center. Fee collection will be handled by the officers of First Episcopal Church.

PROGRAM ADMINISTRATION/MANAGEMENT

A full-time head teacher will be responsible for the day-to-day management of the day care program, intake of children into the program, curriculum design and implementation, daily scheduling of activities, ordering of supplies and equipment, and supervision of staff and volunteers.

The head teacher will be directly responsible to the day care center advisory board. This board will be composed of representatives from the education and health professions, the Germantown community, and First Episcopal Church. The Board will meet on a monthly basis or at such times as may be necessary to make decisions and/or set policy for the day care program. The Advisory Board will, in turn, be responsible to the congregation and pastor of First Episcopal Church. An annual report on the status of the day care program covering all related fiscal matters will be submitted to the Church membership and the appropriate funding sources by the Advisory Board.

PROGRAM STAFFING

The staff of the day care program will include the following personnel: one full-time head teacher, one full-time teacher assistant, and one part-time teacher aide. In addition, the staff of the day care center will be supplemented by the volunteer services of members of First Episcopal Church and the Germantown community. The staff-child ratio is determined in accordance with the day care regulations of the Commonwealth of Pennsylvania.

The staff of the day care center will be selected by the Advisory Board or by a Board-appointed committee. Job descriptions will be developed and qualifications further deliniated by the Advisory Board. Staff will be expected to participate in in-service training and attend local conferences and workshops on early childhood education and child development.

The qualifications, responsibilities, and hours of the volunteers utilized by the center will be determined by the head teacher and approved by the Advisory Board in accordance with the ongoing needs of the day care program.

PROGRAM COMPONENTS

The components of the day care program will include:

The Educational Component. This component consists of lessons, activities, and environmental conditions geared toward the development of aspects of physical, social-emotional, and cognitive growth appropriate for the individual child. These will be implemented via the use of themes or units of study aimed at the development of specific concepts or skills such as parts of the body, the family, shape recognition, plants and animals, etc.

The Social Services Component. This aspect is designed to provide support and make referrals to appropriate agencies that assist with various child and family-related problems. It will rely heavily on a network of community resources to be developed and maintained by the Advisory Board and the day care center staff.

The Health/Nutrition Component. This element is geared toward upgrading and maintaining the general health of the children in the program via the use of community health services and the implementation of a health education program aimed at children and their families. While children will bring lunches from home, suggested lunchbox menus will be posted regularly at the center, along with information on the portions and nutritional needs of the preschool child. A midmorning and midafternoon snack will be served daily.

The Parent/Community Involvement Component. This multifaceted component is aimed at maximizing parent and family participation in the day care program via parent-child activities and special events, as well as parent-teacher meetings. The latter are to be held on a monthly basis. In addition, community resources will be utilized to enhance the quality of all aspects of the program: volunteer services; educational, health and social-services components; and staff selection and training.

PROGRAM EVALUATION

While evaluation of the day care program will be ongoing through stated goals and objectives, other assessment tools will also be utilized.

At the end of the first year of operation, the program will also be evaluated to ascertain the need and desirability of program expansion. The number of applications for admission to the program, space availability, and other factors will be considered at that time. Additionally, parents utilizing the day care center will be surveyed to establish the success of the program in meeting child and family needs.

The annual report submitted by the Advisory Board will detail all of the above information and include data on fiscal matters such as expenditures and plans/projections for the upcoming year.

Figure 3–8 SAMPLE MINIGRANT PROPOSAL (continued)

BUDGET

Category I Administrative and General Costs

A. Salaries and Wages

NO. OF PERSONS	*POSITION*	*MOS. TO BE EMPLOYED*	*BASIS FOR COST*	*ITEM COST*
______	Head Teacher	12	@ ______	$ ______
______	Teacher Assistant	12	______	______
______	Teacher Aide (part-time)	12	______	______
			Subtotal	$ ______

B. Fringe Benefits (at 25% of total salaries and wages)

Social Security (FICA)	@ 6%	______
Health Insurance	8%	______
Retirement	8%	______
Unemployment Compensation	2%	______
Workman's Compensation	1%	______
	Subtotal	$ ______
	TOTAL FOR CATEGORY I	$ ______

Category II Operating Costs

ITEM	*BASIS FOR COST*	*ITEM COST*
Office Supplies	@ ______	$ ______
School Insurance	______	______
Telephone	______	______
Field Trips	______	______
TOTAL FOR CATEGORY II		$ ______

Category III Food/Nutrition Services

Cost for Two Snacks at $____/Day × ____ Children × ____ days

TOTAL FOR CATEGORY III $ ______

Figure 3–8 SAMPLE MINIGRANT PROPOSAL (continued)

Category IV Equipment and Materials

A. Outdoor Play Equipment

1 Climber $ ________

2 Play Balls @ $____ ________

3 Tricycles @ $____ ________

2 Wagons @ $____ ________

Subtotal $ ________

B. Instructional Materials

1 Flannel Board @ $____ $ ________

4 Flannel Board Stories @ $____ ________

1 Tape Recorder ________

1 doz. Audio Cassette Tapes @ $____ ________

1 doz. Story Books @ $____ ________

1 set Rhythm Instruments ________

1 Record Player ________

1 doz. Records @ $____ ________

Subtotal $ ________

C. Furniture

2 Locker Units @ $____ $ ________

2 Tables @ $____ ________

15 Stacking Chairs @ $____ ________

15 Sleeping Cots @ $____ ________

1 Area Rug @ $____ ________

Subtotal $ ________

D. Manipulative Equipment

12 Puzzles @ $____ $ ________

2 Lotto Games @ $____ ________

2 Stringing Beads @ $____ ________

1 Set Duplo Blocks ________

2 Puzzle Racks @ $____ ________

1 Shape Sorter ________

2 Peg Boards @ $____ ________

2 Pounding Benches @ $____ ________

Subtotal $ ________

E. Indoor Play Equipment

1 Wood Rocking Boat $ ________

1 set Hardwood Blocks ________

1 Water/Sand Table with cover ________

Ironing Board with Iron	________
1 Doll Bed	________
3 Dolls @ $____	________
1 Stove	________
1 Sink	________
1 Cabinet/ Refrigerator	________
2 Folding Mats @ $____	________
1 Stand-Up Mirror	________
1 set Family Puppets	________
2 Ride Em Trucks @ $____	________
Subtotal	$ ________

F. Art Supplies

2 doz. Tempera Paint @ $____	________
3 doz. Crayons @ $____	________
1 doz. Paint Brushes @ $____	________
2 doz. Finger Paints @ $____	________
5 Watercolor Sets @ $____	________
20 pkgs. Construction Paper	________
4 pkgs. Finger-Paint Paper	________
2 doz. Elmer's Glue @ $____	________
2 doz. Blunt Scissors @ $____	________
2 Double Easels @ $____	________
Subtotal	$ ________

TOTAL FOR CATEGORY IV $________

Category V Code Conformity (Renovations)

Carpentry, insulation, brickwork, etc. (see estimate from Bob Jones, Builder)	$ ________
Electrical Work (see estimate from L. O. Smith & Sons)	________
Plumbing (see attached estimate)	________
Installation of New Windows	________
TOTAL FOR CATEGORY V	$ ________
BUDGET TOTAL	$ ________

Figure 3–8 SAMPLE MINIGRANT PROPOSAL (continued)

BUDGET SUMMARY

CATEGORY I	Administrative and General Costs	$ ________
CATEGORY II	Operating Costs	________
CATEGORY III	Food/Nutrition Services	________
CATEGORY IV	Equipment and Materials	________
CATEGORY V	Code Conformity (Renovations)	________
	TOTAL COSTS FOR PROGRAM*	$ ________

*An estimated $ ________ is considered "one-time" costs necessary in this budget for permanent equipment and renovations required for conformity with day care regulations.

Figure 3–9

FUND-RAISING LETTER

Dear Friend:

We are pleased to extend our invitation to you and members of your family to attend our 1990 Tom Thumb Pageant so that you may see how your untiring efforts and contributions have helped us improve out building project. The Tom Thumb Pageant continues to be a major program to help us achieve our goal of providing "free tuition" for needy and deserving children who have been identified by our Search and Help Committee as being qualified according to center guidelines.

We definitely would like to have you present to support this, our Fourth Annual Tom Thumb Pageant. If you will be able to attend, please provide us with information on the enclosed form. This will enable us to plan our program, including a special acknowledgement of our families and supporters. We especially look forward to your attendance as a repeating honoree. Networking with friends, supporters, and day care families will allow you an opportunity to renew friendships.

We look forward to hearing from you by ______________________
(Date)

Since the pageant is a fundraiser and naturally involves promotion expenses, we sincerely regret that we cannot provide a free ticket for you. Your understanding is greatly appreciated.

Very sincerely yours,

____
(Name of Chairperson)

Figure 3–10

EXAMPLES OF FUND-RAISING ACTIVITIES

1. BOOK SALE

BOOK SALE SET TODAY TO FINANCE "DAY CENTER NEWSLETTER"

Books on early childhood education, games, toys, magazines, and computer programs for preschoolers are among the offerings in today's book sale.

- Prices are reasonable and affordable. Purchases may be paid for with cash and major credit cards. The Day Care Center will receive an added bonus for purchases paid by using the ________________ credit card.
- This sale is sponsored by the Grant Day Care Parents' Association in conjunction with Greene Street Publishers. Hours are from 10 A.M. to 6 P.M. in the Instructional Materials Center.

2. RUMMAGE AND BAKE SALE

There will be a rummage and bake sale from 10 A.M. to 8 P.M. Friday, May 6, and from 9 A.M. to 3 P.M. Saturday, May 7, at Grant Day Care Association. The Day Care Center needs articles to be donated for sale. Please bring brown-paper bags.

3. CAR WASH

The Preschool Support Group is having a car wash from 10 A.M. to 4 P.M. Saturday, April 10, at the Lincoln Garage, 235 Main Street. Donations $3.00, cars cleaned both inside and out.

Figure 3–11

THANK-YOU LETTER FOR DONATED GOODS AND SERVICES

Dear ______________________________
(Name)

Throughout the short history of Grant Day Care Association it has been apparent that volunteers have played a unique part in the success of our program. That fact was especially evident during the recent, successfully completed, Third Annual Book Fair and Carnival.

Our volunteers were simply marvelous in carrying out assignments from the most menial task to serving in high-profile activities. It was heartwarming to see the responsiveness that each and every one displayed in doing their very best.

Thanks for your determination to take on a multitude of tasks so willingly and tenaciously without a thought of personal gain or recognition. Your efforts serve as a beacon for others to follow, leading to an overwhelming financial and entertainment success.

I sincerely hope that you feel the gut-level satisfaction that accompanies knowing that you have done a good job and that all those laborious hours, seemingly back-breaking in some instances, were well worth the effort.

Thank you for an outstanding job. And remember, we expect you back next year to lead us to further success and glory.

Sincerely,

Alyson Johns
Director

Further Reading

CONNORS, T.D., *The Non-Profit Organization Handbook*. New York: McGraw-Hill, 1980.

DANIELS, C.E. *A Budget Primer and Worksheets for Proposal Writers*. Washington, DC: Federal Resources Advisory Service, Association of American Colleges, 1979.

EVANS, E.B., and G.E. SAIA. *Day Care For Infants*. Boston: Beacon Press, 1972.

GRIFFIN, A. *How to Start and Operate a Day Care Home*. Chicago: Henry Regnery, 1973.

MCCOREY, H., and D. MCCOREY. *The Business of Family Day Care*. Santa Monica, CA: Roundtable Publishing, 1988.

MILLER, J.A, and S. WEISSMAN. *The Parent's Guide to Daycare*. New York: Bantam Books, 1986.

MURPHY, K. *A House Full of Kids*. Boston: Beacon Press, 1984.

STREETS, D.T. *Administering Day Care and Preschool Programs*. Boston: Allyn and Bacon, 1982.

WARREN, P.B. *The Dynamics of Funding: An Educator's Guide to Effective Grantsmanship*. Boston: Allyn and Bacon, 1980.

Booklets and Pamphlets

Analyzing Costs in a Residential Group Care Facility. Child Welfare League of America, Inc., 67 Irving Place, New York, New York 10003, 116 pages. For administrators and accountants: an in-depth study of all control factors.

Determining Fees for Day Care Services. U.S. Department of Health, Education and Welfare, Children's Bureau, Washington, D.C. 20201, 14 pages, free. Covers the use of sliding and maximum fees, periodic evaluation of fees set, with examples of various methods for working out costs of services as well as setting fees.

section 4

PERSONNEL SUPERVISION & STAFF DEVELOPMENT

The forms and exhibits in Section 4 relate to the most significant element in any child care program—the staff. Teachers and caregivers' influence and impact on the development of young children is far greater than that of educational methodology or a particular curriculum. Program direction, supervision, and provision of day care services are functions forecasted by center staff, regardless of the size of the center. Whether the center is designed to provide full-day, comprehensive day care services or custodial care, its purpose will affect the selection of the staff. Staffing will be subjected to annual reviews as a yardstick of that purpose.

BASIC STAFFING CONCERNS

Staffing considerations deserve thoughtful deliberation. Four primary issues form the basis of any serious discussion of staffing concerns: (1) the number of staff members required for a quality program (the staff-child ratio), (2) the qualifications expected of staff members, (3) recognition of competency and performance, and (4) constancy of care. These issues are important for small and large centers alike and are reflected to various degrees in the sample advertisements for staff positions shown in Figure 4–1.

The Director

The director of a day care program must be someone with basic knowledge of child development and children's needs. It is important that he or she be a competent administrator as well. The director is expected to know how to formulate child care policy decisions deliberated with parent advisory committees, boards of directors, parent volunteers, and staff; ensure requirements for health and safety standards are met; hire and dismiss staff; supervise and evaluate staff performance; provide for nutrition and mental health needs; plan for parent and volunteer involvement; network with community agencies; secure adequate funding and observe budget limitations; recruit children; and conduct orientation and in-service training programs for staff development.

This partial list clearly demonstrates the wide range of functions that are the responsibilities of the director. An exceptionally competent person is required to fulfill all of those responsibilities equally well. Knowing which of these administrative tasks to delegate to other support and consultative staff (in large centers) is extremely important to the director. The job obviously requires a person with both experience and ability as well as an academic degree in early childhood education or child development, or experiences and work qualifications equivalent to such formal training. Some states require that the director be a college graduate with a degree in early childhood education or a related field.

Program Staff

A conscious decision must be made by the administration to attract and retain a well-qualified staff committed to providing a quality program for children. The personnel selection process should include such key documented information on staff qualifications and center requirements as: (1) education and training, work history, current health status, credentials or licenses, and supplemental skills (special talents and skills, languages spoken proficiently); (2) orientation program for all newly hired employees and volunteers; (3) training opportunities for all staff members (both in-service and those conducted by early childhood education consultants); (4) regularly scheduled performance appraisals; (5) whenever possible, well-defined career ladders; and (6) commitment from staff and administration to the continuation of staff members' education and training in an effort to improve their competence.

Figures 4–2 through 4–12 provide a variety of useful tools for hiring and orientation of staff. These include a sample employment application (Figure 4–2) and three forms for checking into a candidate's background: Application for Child Abuse History (Figure 4–3), Request for Criminal History Record Information (Figure 4–4), and Employment Eligibility Verification (Figure 4–5). Also provided are two interviewing aids, Sample Interview Questionnaire (Figure 4–6), and Employment Candidate Observation Rating Form (Figure 4–7), a sample contract (Figure 4–8), New Personnel Orientation Agenda (Figure 4–9), an employee health examination form (Figure 4–10), an employee time sheet (Figure 4–11), and a job description for a teacher aide (Figure 4–12).

TRAINING AND DEVELOPMENT

The staff may be asked by the director to provide input regarding training needs. This method of securing training-needs information often serves as a forum for staff members to provide feedback on their own development. The director/administrator may also use a variety of tools when evaluating teacher performance, for example, that shown in Figure 4–13, "Day Care Center Staff Evaluation." National and local as well as individual-center designed competencies list behavioral indicators or qualifications important for working with young children. Training topics may be formulated after observations and individual meetings with staff have taken place.

For the staff, the training component can mean the difference between job satisfaction and stress or creativity and stagnation. Administrative support may well be viewed as an intangible fringe benefit that serves as an indicator that individual contributions and meritorious service are both important and recognized. Also, the challenge of functioning as a creative and productive facilitator of children's learning is a powerful motivator. Staff members take more pride in their abilities, and the children they serve benefit.

Figure 4–1

SAMPLE ADVERTISEMENTS FOR STAFF POSITIONS

Sample 1: Teacher/Director

Talented take-charge person for infant-toddler unit in large day care center. Supervise staff, develop curriculum, work directly with children, and interface with parents. Salary and benefits.

Sample 2: Teacher

Early childhood educator with state certification, small group, health and dental benefits.

Sample 3: Teacher

Responsible for classroom of three and four year olds, BS or AA in Early Childhood Education. Bilingual (Spanish), bicultural preferred. Send resume to Community Head Start, Head Start Center Director.

Sample 4: Director

A large public agency has an immediate need for a Head Start Center Director. This is administrative management work that includes operating a Head Start Center and establishing and maintaining a comprehensive and interdisciplinary program for prekindergarten children and their families. Requirements include successful completion of a Master's degree program at an accredited college or university with major coursework in early childhood education or child development. Four years experience in Head Start or related programs, three years of which will have been in an administrative or supervisory capacity, is also required.

Excellent compensation with benefit package including medical, dental, vision, and prescription plans, three weeks vacation, generous holidays, and paid personal leave.

Send resume with cover letter detailing qualifications by January 7 to Head Start Center Director Search Committee.

Figure 4–2

SAMPLE EMPLOYMENT APPLICATION
GRANT DAY CARE ASSOCIATION

Name ____
Last First MI Soc. Sec. #

Address ____
Number (Apt) Street City, State, Zip

Telephone No. ____
Home Business

Position Desired ____

EDUCATION HISTORY

High School ____
From To Name and Location Major Year Graduated Degree

College ____
From To Name and Location Major Year Graduated Degree

Other (Specify) ____
From To Name and Location Major Year Graduated Degree

CREDENTIALS OR CERTIFICATES HELD

List courses of study or training earned in Early Childhood Education, Child Development, and Elementary Education ______________________________

____

Figure 4–2 SAMPLE EMPLOYMENT APPLICATION (continued)

EXPERIENCE

1. ____
From To Name and Address of Employer Position Salary Reason for Leaving

2. ____
From To Name and Address of Employer Position Salary Reason for Leaving

3. ____
From To Name and Address of Employer Position Salary Reason for Leaving

REFERENCES: List the names of three persons related to you whom you have known at least one year through community involvement.

1. ____
Name Address Business Telephone

2. ____
Name Address Business Telephone

3. ____
Name Address Business Telephone

Professional Affiliations

____

____

____

____

Signature of Applicant ______________________________

Figure 4–3

PENNSYLVANIA CHILD ABUSE HISTORY CLEARANCE

INSTRUCTIONS: Complete Section I only. Please print clearly in ink. Enclose check or money order for $10.00 payable to Department of Public Welfare. **DO NOT SEND CASH.** Applications received without fee will not be processed. Send to Department of Public Welfare, P.O. Box 8170, Harrisburg, PA 17105-8170

SECTION I - APPLICANT IDENTIFICATION
(Indicate Reason For Requesting Clearance (Check ONE Block Only)

1. ☐ EMPLOYMENT
2. ☐ ADOPTION
3. ☐ FOSTER CARE
4. ☐ VOLUNTARY — A copy of your Request for Criminal History Record Information (Form SP4-164) must be attached. Out-of-State residents must also attach a copy of their FBI Clearance (Form FD-258).
5. ☐ CWEP (Community Work Experience Program Participant)

Signature of Confirming CAO Representative ______ CAO Telephone No. ______

CHILDLINE USE ONLY
DATE RECEIVED BY CHILDLINE

RETURN ADDRESS BLOCK – PLEASE PRINT CLEARLY

NAME

STREET — APT. NO. BOX NO.

CITY, STATE — ZIP CODE

IN THE BLOCK ABOVE, ENTER FULL NAME OF APPLICANT. DO NOT USE INITIALS. ALSO ENTER ENTIRE CURRENT ADDRESS.

SOCIAL SECURITY NO. ▶ — —	
AGE	DATE OF BIRTH
SEX ☐ M ☐ F	COUNTY OF CURRENT RESIDENCE
LENGTH OF TIME AT CURRENT ADDRESS	▶ ______ YRS. ______ MOS.
DAYTIME TELEPHONE NO.	▶ ( )

OTHER NAMES USED BY APPLICANT SINCE 1975 (Include Maiden Name, Nicknames, Aliases) (First, Middle, Last)

1.	2.

FORMER ADDRESSES OF APPLICANT (from November 1975 up to, but not including, current address) Include approximate dates you resided at each address. List Street, Apt. No., Box No., City, State, County, & Zip Code. For military service list City, State, and/or Country where stationed. Attach additional pages if necessary.

Address	Dates	Address	Dates
1.	MO/YR TO MO/YR	3.	MO/YR TO MO/YR
2.	MO/YR TO MO/YR	4.	MO/YR TO MO/YR

MEMBERS OF APPLICANT'S HOUSEHOLD (Include all persons who currently reside with you or who have resided with you at any of your former addresses.) Attach additional pages if necessary.

NAME (First, Middle, Last, do not use initials)	RELATIONSHIP TO APPLICANT	AGE	SEX
1.			
2.			
3.			
4.			
5.			
6.			

I certify that the above information is accurate and complete to the best of my knowledge and belief and submitted as true and correct under penalty of law (Section 4904 of the Pennsylvania Crimes Code).

Applicant's Signature ______ Date ______

SECTION II - RESULTS OF HISTORY CHECK - Childline Use Only

☐ APPLICANT **IS NOT** LISTED IN THE STATEWIDE CENTRAL REGISTER AS A PERPETRATOR OF CHILD ABUSE.

☐ APPLICANT **IS** LISTED IN THE STATEWIDE CENTRAL REGISTER AS A PERPETRATOR OF CHILD ABUSE. (SEE BELOW.)

REPORTS IDENTIFIED

	STATUS	DATE OF INCIDENT		STATUS	DATE OF INCIDENT
1.			3.		
2.			4.		

VERIFIER ______ DATE ______ VERIFIER'S SUPERVISOR ______ DATE ______

01143A — APPLICATION — CY 113 - 12/88

Figure 4–3 APPLICATION FOR CHILD ABUSE HISTORY (continued)

SPECIAL NOTES

DUE TO THE NATURE AND CONFIDENTIALITY OF THE INFORMATION REQUESTED, CHILD ABUSE CLEARANCES MUST BE RETURNED DIRECTLY TO THE APPLICANT.

BEFORE MAILING YOUR APPLICATION TO THE DEPARTMENT OF PUBLIC WELFARE, PLEASE MAKE ONE COPY AND GIVE TO YOUR EMPLOYER IF YOU ARE BEING HIRED ON A PROVISIONAL BASIS.

YOUR ORIGINAL PENNSYLVANIA CHILD ABUSE HISTORY CLEARANCE WILL BE RETURNED TO YOU WITH AN OFFICIAL SIGNATURE IN SECTION II. HAVE A COPY OF THE CLEARANCE MADE AND GIVE THE COPY TO THE AGENCY TO RETAIN IN ITS FILE. THE AGENCY MUST ALSO VIEW THE ORIGINAL BUT THE APPLICANT RETAINS THE ORIGINAL.

SECTION III - VOLUNTARY CERTIFICATION - Childline Use Only

________________________________ has requested a certification which includes a clearance of his/her name against the child abuse and criminal history files.

The results of the child abuse history clearance are listed in Section II on the reverse side. The results of the criminal history clearance(s) is (are) listed below. Out-of-state residents must have criminal history clearance from both the Pennsylvania State Police and the FBI. The voluntary certification may be obtained every two years.

It is the responsibility of parents and guardians to review this information to determine the suitability of the applicant as a substitute caregiver.

PENNSYLVANIA CHILD ABUSE HISTORY CLEARANCE

- ☐ Applicant is named as the perpetrator of a "Founded" child abuse report which occurred in the last five years.
- ☐ Applicant is named as the perpetrator of a "Founded" child abuse report which occurred over five years ago.
- ☐ Applicant is named as the perpetrator of an "Indicated" child abuse report.
- ☐ Applicant is not named as the perpetrator of any child abuse reports contained in the Statewide Central Register.

PENNSYLVANIA STATE POLICE CLEARANCE

- ☐ Record exists and contains convictions which prohibit hire in a child care position. Report attached.
- ☐ Record exists, but convictions do not prohibit hire in a child care position. Report attached.
- ☐ Record exists, but convictions are beyond the five year limit and do not prohibit hire in a child care position. Report attached.
- ☐ No record exists. Report attached.

FBI CLEARANCE

- ☐ Record exists and contains convictions which prohibit hire in a child care position. Report attached.
- ☐ Record exists, but convictions do not prohibit hire in a child care position. Report attached.
- ☐ Record exists, but convictions are beyond the five year limit and do not prohibit hire in a child care position. Report attached.
- ☐ Record exists, but no convictions are shown. This does not prohibit hire in a child care position.
- ☐ No record exists. Report attached.

VERIFIER	DATE	VERIFIER'S SUPERVISOR	DATE

CY 113 - 12/88 011438

Figure 4–4

SP 4 - 164 (2-88)

FOR CENTRAL REPOSITORY USE ONLY (LEAVE BLANK)

PENNSYLVANIA STATE POLICE

REQUEST FOR CRIMINAL HISTORY RECORD INFORMATION

(SEE REVERSE SIDE FOR INSTRUCTIONS)

TYPE OR PRINT ONLY

PART I TO BE COMPLETED BY REQUESTER — DATE OF REQUEST

NAME (Last) (First) (Middle)

MAIDEN NAME AND/OR ALIASES | SOCIAL SECURITY NO. | DATE OF BIRTH | SEX | RACE

REQUESTER IDENTIFICATION

☐ CRIMINAL JUSTICE AGENCY - FEE EXEMPT
☐ NONCRIMINAL JUSTICE AGENCY - FEE EXEMPT
☐ INDIVIDUAL - NONCRIMINAL JUSTICE AGENCY - $10 FEE ENCLOSED

REASON FOR REQUEST

☐ CRIMINAL INVESTIGATION
☐ INDIVIDUAL ACCESS AND REVIEW BY SUBJECT OF RECORD OR LEGAL REPRESENTATIVE
☐ CRIMINAL JUSTICE EMPLOYMENT
☐ NONCRIMINAL JUSTICE EMPLOYMENT
☐ COURT REQUEST ON PRIOR ARD
☐ OTHER (Specify) ______

PART II TO BE COMPLETED BY CRIMINAL JUSTICE AGENCIES ONLY

INFORMATION REQUESTED

☐ FINGERPRINTS
☐ RAP SHEET ☐ PHOTO ☐ PRIOR ARD

SID NO. (If available) | OTN OR OCA NO. (If available)

PART III FOR CENTRAL REPOSITORY USE ONLY (LEAVE BLANK)

INFORMATION DISSEMINATED

☐ NO RECORD OR NO RECORD THAT MEETS DISSEMINATION CRITERIA
☐ RAP SHEET ☐ FINGERPRINTS ☐ PHOTO

SID NO.

INQUIRY BY | DISSEMINATION BY

THE INFORMATION FURNISHED BY THE CENTRAL REPOSITORY IS SOLELY BASED ON THE FOLLOWING IDENTIFIERS THAT MATCH THOSE FURNISHED BY THE REQUESTER:

☐ SID NO. ☐ DATE OF BIRTH ☐ RACE
☐ OTN/OCA NO. ☐ MAIDEN NAME ☐ SEX
☐ NAME ☐ SOCIAL SECURITY NO. ☐ ALIAS

Director, Central Repository

Response based on comparison of requester furnished information and/or fingerprints against a name index and/or fingerprints contained in the files of the Pennsylvania State Police Central Repository only, and does not preclude the existence of other criminal records which may be contained in the repositories of other local, state or federal criminal justice agencies.

PART IV TO BE COMPLETED BY REQUESTER

NAME OF INDIVIDUAL MAKING REQUEST ______

REQUEST TO BE MAILED TO:

NAME

ADDRESS

CITY STATE ZIP CODE

LIST TELEPHONE NO. TO BE USED IN CASE OF PROBLEM.

INCLUDE AREA CODE

Figure 4–5

EMPLOYMENT ELIGIBILITY VERIFICATION (Form I-9)

1 EMPLOYEE INFORMATION AND VERIFICATION: (To be completed and signed by employee.)

Name: (Print or Type) Last	First	Middle	Birth Name
Address: Street Name and Number	City	State	ZIP Code
Date of Birth (Month/Day/Year)		Social Security Number	

I attest, under penalty of perjury, that I am (check a box):

☐ 1. A citizen or national of the United States.
☐ 2. An alien lawfully admitted for permanent residence (Alien Number A ________).
☐ 3. An alien authorized by the Immigration and Naturalization Service to work in the United States (Alien Number A ________, or Admission Number ________, expiration of employment authorization, if any ________).

I attest, under penalty of perjury, the documents that I have presented as evidence of identity and employment eligibility are genuine and relate to me. I am aware that federal law provides for imprisonment and/or fine for any false statements or use of false documents in connection with this certificate.

Signature	Date (Month/Day/Year)

PREPARER/TRANSLATOR CERTIFICATION (To be completed if prepared by person other than the employee). I attest, under penalty of perjury, that the above was prepared by me at the request of the named individual and is based on all information of which I have any knowledge.

Signature	Name (Print or Type)		
Address (Street Name and Number)	City	State	Zip Code

2 EMPLOYER REVIEW AND VERIFICATION: (To be completed and signed by employer.)

Instructions:
Examine one document from List A and check the appropriate box, ***OR*** examine one document from List B ***and*** one from List C and check the appropriate boxes. Provide the ***Document Identification Number*** and ***Expiration Date*** for the document checked.

List A Documents that Establish Identity and Employment Eligibility	List B Documents that Establish Identity		List C Documents that Establish Employment Eligibility
☐ 1. United States Passport ☐ 2. Certificate of United States Citizenship ☐ 3. Certificate of Naturalization ☐ 4. Unexpired foreign passport with attached Employment Authorization ☐ 5. Alien Registration Card with photograph	☐ 1. A State-issued driver's license or a State-issued I.D. card with a photograph, or information, including name, sex, date of birth, height, weight, and color of eyes. (Specify State) ________) ☐ 2. U.S. Military Card ☐ 3. Other (Specify document and issuing authority) ________	**and**	☐ 1. Original Social Security Number Card (other than a card stating it is not valid for employment) ☐ 2. A birth certificate issued by State, county, or municipal authority bearing a seal or other certification ☐ 3. Unexpired INS Employment Authorization Specify form # ________
Document Identification # ________	***Document Identification*** # ________		***Document Identification*** # ________
Expiration Date (if any) ________	***Expiration Date (if any)*** ________		***Expiration Date (if any)*** ________

CERTIFICATION: I attest, under penalty of perjury, that I have examined the documents presented by the above individual, that they appear to be genuine and to relate to the individual named, and that the individual, to the best of my knowledge, is eligible to work in the United States.

Signature	Name (Print or Type)	Title
Employer Name	Address	Date

Form I-9 (05/07/87)
OMB No. 1115-0136

U.S. Department of Justice
Immigration and Naturalization Service

Figure 4–5 EMPLOYMENT ELIGIBILITY VERIFICATION (continued)

Employment Eligibility Verification

NOTICE: Authority for collecting the information on this form is in Title 8, United States Code, Section 1324A, which requires employers to verify employment eligibility of individuals on a form approved by the Attorney General. This form will be used to verify the individual's eligibility for employment in the United States. Failure to present this form for inspection to officers of the Immigration and Naturalization Service or Department of Labor within the time period specified by regulation, or improper completion or retention of this form, may be a violation of the above law and may result in a civil money penalty.

Section 1. Instructions to Employee/Preparer for completing this form

Instructions for the employee.

All employees, upon being hired, must complete Section 1 of this form. Any person hired after November 6, 1986 must complete this form. (For the purpose of completion of this form the term "hired" applies to those employed, recruited or referred for a fee.)

All employees must print or type their complete name, address, date of birth, and Social Security Number. The block which correctly indicates the employee's immigration status must be checked. If the second block is checked, the employee's Alien Registration Number must be provided. If the third block is checked, the employee's Alien Registration Number ***or*** Admission Number must be provided, as well as the date of expiration of that status, if it expires.

All employees whose present names differ from birth names, because of marriage or other reasons, must print or type their birth names in the appropriate space of Section 1. Also, employees whose names change after employment verification should report these changes to their employer.

All employees must sign and date the form.

Instructions for the preparer of the form, if not the employee.

If a person assists the employee with completing this form, the preparer must certify the form by signing it and printing or typing his or her complete name and address.

Section 2. Instructions to Employer for completing this form

(For the purpose of completion of this form, the term "employer" applies to employers and those who recruit or refer for a fee.)

Employers must complete this section by examining evidence of identity and employment eligibility, and:

- checking the appropriate box in List A ***or*** boxes in both Lists B and C;
- recording the document identification number and expiration date (if any);
- recording the type of form if not specifically identified in the list;
- signing the certification section.

NOTE: Employers are responsible for reverifying employment eligibility of employees whose employment eligibility documents carry an expiration date.

Copies of documentation presented by an individual for the purpose of establishing identity and employment eligibility may be copied and retained for the purpose of complying with the requirements of this form and no other purpose. Any copies of documentation made for this purpose should be maintained with this form.

Name changes of employees which occur after preparation of this form should be recorded on the form by lining through the old name, printing the new name and the reason (such as marriage), and dating and initialing the changes. Employers should not attempt to delete or erase the old name in any fashion.

RETENTION OF RECORDS.

The completed form must be retained by the employer for:

- three years after the date of hiring; or
- one year after the date the employment is terminated, whichever is later.

Employers may photocopy or reprint this form as necessary.

U.S. Department of Justice
Immigration and Naturalization Service

OMB #1115-0136
Form I-9 (05/07/87)

Figure 4–6

SAMPLE INTERVIEW QUESTIONNAIRE

Candidate Name ______________________________ Date __________

1. What kind of physical environment is important for young children's classrooms? Social? Emotional?

2. Tell us why you decided to become a child care worker?

3. What strengths will you bring to the position of Teacher/Caregiver? Head Teacher? Aide? etc.

4. Tell us what you would do if a child . . .

5. Tell us what you want to be doing professionally in three years.

Figure 4–7

EMPLOYMENT CANDIDATE OBSERVATION RATING FORM

Name ______________________ Date ____________

Position ______________________

	1	2	3	4	5
1. Appearance					
2. Clarity of expression					
3. Flexibility					
4. Initiative					
5. Relationship with children					
6. Relationship with staff					
7. Competence, knowledge, skill					
8. Reaction to supervision					
9. Personality					
10. Judgment, alertness					
Training					
Experience					

Recommendation:

Employ ______________________

Do Not Employ ______________________

Reasons: ______________________

____

____

____

Interviewer's Name ______________________

Rating Scale:

1 = Excellent
2 = Good
3 = Fair
4 = Poor
5 = Unsatisfactory

Figure 4–8

EMPLOYMENT CONTRACT

This employment contract is made between ______________________
Name of Employee

and ______________________________________ whose address is
Name of Provider

____
Address of Child Care Center City State Zip

The duties for the position of Child Care Aide set forth by this agreement are (1) to maintain simple records; (2) to assist Teacher by working with children singly and in groups; (3) to prepare materials and learning centers; (4) to assist in directing and coordinating activities of volunteers, (5) to participate in and guide activities for the social-emotional, physical, cognitive, and nutritional development of children; and (6) to perform related duties as specified by the Center Director.

The work schedule will consist of 40 hours per week. Breaks of 15 minutes are authorized for one morning and one afternoon period. Lunch will be taken with the children.

All employees are entitled to a two-week paid vacation that will be scheduled according to Center needs.

The Center will be closed on the following holidays: New Year's Day, Martin Luther King's Birthday, Independence Day, Memorial Day, Thanksgiving Day, Christmas Day. These are paid staff holidays.

All employees will present evidence of the required police check for history of child abuse, request for criminal history record, and immunization and health records prior to starting date for work.

The Center will provide you with a detailed copy of the Personnel Policies, including job description, attendance requirements, grievance procedures, pay ranges, and fringe benefits. Read the Policies carefully before being hired and *accept employment only* with the understanding that you *accept the conditions* set forth in the Policies.

A written 2-week notice is required when you terminate employment.

This Contract shall be renewed annually on the anniversary of your employment or its nearest date.

Figure 4–9

NEW PERSONNEL ORIENTATION AGENDA
ORIENTATION FOR NEW TEACHER AIDES

I. **Welcome**
   A. Introductions
   B. Review of schedule events

II. **Lecture**
   The philosophy and goals of the Center, including policy, procedures, and organization

III. **Distribution of Orientation Manual**

IV. **The Roles and Responsibilities of the Teacher Aides**

V. **Center Rules and Regulations**
   A. Attendance requirements
   B. Notification of absences
   C. Policy on corporal punishment
   D. Dress codes
   E. Smoking regulations
   F. Other pertinent rules/regulations

VI. **Professional Behavior Regarding Confidentiality**
   Legal and ethical restraints

VII. **Grievance Procedures**

VIII. **The Team Concept in Education**

IX. **Competencies Expected**

X. **Supervision**
   Role of Director/Supervisor and the type of supervision new employee can expect

XI. **Question and Answer Period**

Figure 4–10

EMPLOYEE HEALTH EXAMINATION FORM

Employee Completes

Date ______________

Name of Employee ____

Address of Employee ____

Telephone Number ______________

Employer's Address ____

Telephone Number ______________

To Be Completed By Health Professional

Weight __________ Height __________ Blood Pressure ______________

Do you consider these normal for this patient? ___________________

Vision ______________________ (Corrected by glasses?)

Hearing ____________________

Chest X-Ray ______________

Tuberculin Test ____________

Heart ______________________

Chest ______________________

Epilepsy? __________________

Diabetes? __________________

Figure 4–10 EMPLOYEE HEALTH EXAMINATION FORM (continued)

Immunization Status (measles, mumps, DPT) ______________________

Drug or Alcohol Dependency? ______________________

Please note any special medical problem requiring limitations on activity or medication, or that might affect patient's work role.

Comments/Recommendations ______________________

____

____

____

____

What is your opinion concerning the general health of this patient relative to his or her suitability to work in a preschool?

Excellent ______ Good ______ Fair ______ Questionable ______

Unsatisfactory ______

Name and Address of Physician ______________________

____

____

License Number __________

Signature of Physician ______________________

Telephone Number ____________

Date ____________

Figure 4–11

EMPLOYEE TIME SHEET
GRANT DAY CARE ASSOCIATION

____
Date

Employee Name	Monday In/Out	Tuesday In/Out	Wednesday In/Out	Thursday In/Out	Friday In/Out	Remarks
1.						
2.						
3.						
4.						
5.						
6.						
7.						
8.						
9.						
10.						

V = Vacation
S = Sick Leave
F = Funeral Leave
All leaves must be approved by Center Director

____
Director's Signature

Figure 4–12

STAFF ROLES AND RESPONSIBILITIES
THE TEACHER AIDE

Classroom Organization	Implements plans specified by teacher concerning daily/weekly schedule, individual and group activities for children, lesson plans, room arrangements, and learning centers
Behavior Management	Implements and reinforces the same behavior management strategies utilized by the teacher
Teaching	Assists teacher by working with children singly and in groups
Learning Environment	Prepares materials and learning areas, participates in or guides activities for the social, nutritional, physical, emotional, and academic development of children
Working with Parents	Helps direct activities of volunteers and meets with parents under direction of the teacher
Working with Children	Assists children to be self-reliant and to relate to others. Assists by guiding students or modeling appropriately in the areas of communications and personal hygiene
Other Related Duties	(as needed)

Figure 4–13

DAY CARE CENTER STAFF EVALUATION

Employee Name ____________ Employee Job Title ____________

Soc. Sec. No. ____________

Rater's Name ____________ Rater's Title ____________

Date of Rating ____________

Purpose: This appraisal is an evaluation of a permanent employee's performance and is required annually. This review is designed to aid, improve, and direct employee's performance in a positive manner.

1. Performance Status ____________

2. Recommendations for Improvement ____________

3. Goals/Objectives for Employee ____________

4. Employee Comments ____________

Examples of Performance Criteria

Job Knowledge
Attendance
Written-Communication Skills
Oral-Communication Skills
Interpersonal Skills

Cooperation
Collaboration
Responsibility
Dependability

Interest/Initiative/Motivation
Decision-Making Skills
Goal-Setting Skills
Conflict Resolution
Ability to Accept/Delegate Authority

Management Development Skills
Responsiveness to Training

Employee Signature ____________

Rater's Signature ____________

Figure 4–14

CHECKLIST FOR OBSERVING AND RECORDING TEACHER BEHAVIOR

Directions: Please check the level of response demonstrated by the teacher/caregiver in each of the situations listed below:

	1	2	3	4	5
1. Teacher frequently reminds children of classroom rules (e.g., no pushing, no running, etc.)					
2. Teacher positions self so all areas of the room are easily visible					
3. Teacher checks to see that bathrooms are well supplied with soap, tissues, towels					
4. Teacher makes certain that children brush their teeth					
5. Teacher maintains wall displays at child's eye level					
6. Teacher arranges interest areas, furniture, and equipment to allow for smooth movement of adults and children					
7. Teacher provides opportunities for children to engage in several fine-motor activities during the day (e.g., cutting with scissors, bead stringing, etc.)					
8. Teacher encourages children to participate in gross-motor activity during the day					
9. Teacher supplies science materials for children's use (e.g., rock collections, lenses, shells, plants, small animals, pine cones, etc.)					
10. Teacher provides opportunities for children to engage in cognitive activities (e.g., counting, sorting, matching, etc.)					

Figure 4–14 OBSERVING AND RECORDING TEACHER BEHAVIOR (continued)

	1	2	3	4	5
11. Teacher models appropriate language, speaks clearly and distinctly					
12. Teacher listens attentively to children					
13. Teacher plans the environment to allow for creative expression (e.g., dress-up area, musical instruments, puppets, art supplies, paints, blocks, housekeeping area, etc.)					
14. Teacher encourages children's efforts with verbal reinforcements such as "I like the block house that you built"					
15. Teacher greets each child by name on arrival					
16. Teacher attempts to sit, kneel, or bend at child's level when talking or listening to children					
17. Teacher demonstrates awareness of the importance in utilizing meal and snack time to encourage friendly discussion among children					
18. Teacher reinforces socially acceptable behavior, (i.e., tactful behavior, manners)					
19. Teacher plans for quiet and active routines					
20. Teacher uses gentle reminders of rules to guide children's behavior (e.g., "Use your indoor voices")					

Rating Scale:
1 = Excellent
2 = Good
3 = Satisfactory
4 = Needs Improvement
5 = Unsatisfactory

Further Reading

AXELROD, P. *Preschool and Child Care Administration.* Ann Arbor, MI: The University of Michigan, 1974.

DECKER, C.A. and J.R. DECKER. *Planning and Administering in Early Childhood Programs.* Columbus, OH: Merrill, 1980.

GROSETT, M.D., et al. *So You're Going to Run A Day Care Council!* New York: Day Care Council of New York, 1971.

GROSSMAN, A.H. *Personal Management in Recreation and Leisure Services.* South Plainfield, NJ: Groupwork Today, 1980.

JONES, M.A. "Job Descriptions Made Easy." *Personnel Journal,* May 1984, p. 32.

KIRKPATRICK, D.L. "Effective Supervisory Training and Development, Part I: Responsibility, Needs and Objectives." *Personnel,* November–December 1984.

STREETS, D.T., ed. *Administering Day Care and Preschool Programs.* Boston: Allyn and Bacon, 1982.

ZAND, D.E. *Information, Organization and Power.* New York: McGraw-Hill, 1981.

section 5

PROGRAM PLANNING FOR THE EARLY CHILDHOOD SETTING

Section 5 provides an assortment of management aids for developing effective educational programs for young children. These range from sample goals for early learning to criteria for measuring children's programs.

GROWTH OF EARLY CHILDHOOD EDUCATION

One of several factors which most influenced American education in the second half of this century was the 1957 launching of Sputnik by the U.S.S.R. In the flood of changes in educational methods and approaches that followed came different ways of looking at child development and readiness for learning. As years passed there evolved a widespread acceptance by both professionals and the public that learning did not begin with entry into kindergarten or first grade. Theories developed by Jean Piaget, Erik Erickson, Maria Montessori, and others attracted widespread interest. Researchers and scholars alike supported the notion that cognitive, physical, social, and emotional facets of development were indeed active at birth and throughout the preschool period. Sanction for these beliefs was supplied by the American government with the establishment of the Head Start program in 1964.

Since that time, the number of early childhood programs has multiplied. Today, day care centers, preschool learning programs, parent cooperatives, play groups, and at-home learning programs are among the types of early learning approaches in wide use in the United States. Many of those facilities designed to care for the children of working parents also use a developmental model to facilitate the overall growth of youngsters.

The models of curriculum used in the early childhood field are almost as many and varied as the facilities themselves. There are a range of opinions about which approach is best for young children. However, it is not the purpose here to support the validity of any one model. Rather the goal is to provide an overview of the programming process and the tasks related to it. These tasks include the development of goals and objectives for children; the identification of content areas and concepts to be included in the curriculum; the development of units of study, lessons, activities, and environmental conditions to facilitate learning; selection of materials and equipment for preschool programs; and environmental arrangement. While these topics are only briefly discussed in the narrative part of this section, they are followed by a variety of examples to be used or adapted by readers.

DEVELOPING GOALS AND OBJECTIVES FOR YOUNG CHILDREN

In order for a program to pinpoint its direction, it is essential to establish goals. Goals are statements of the long-term aims of a program. In a well-organized early childhood center there are several sets of goals pertaining to various aspects of the program. There should also be corresponding means of achieving these goals and ways to measure steps made toward them.

Goals for the children's program, those pertaining to curriculum, are generally designed around the basic growth areas of social-emotional, cognitive, language, and physical development, as illustrated in Figure 5–1. These are useful in the annual or semiannual planning conducted by the early childhood staff. Objectives, on the other hand, may also pertain to specific concepts, skills, and content areas, as shown in Figure 5-2. These are useful in the daily development of lesson, activity, and environmental plans.*

When behavioral objectives are developed, they serve as specific indicators of the purposes of the curriculum and also provide indicators of its effectiveness. That is, the behavioral objectives specify what children should be able to do as a result of new learning and the circumstances under which youngsters should be able to demonstrate a new knowledge or skills. Keep in mind that not all children will be able to meet every objective at the ages indicated. Some children will meet developmental aims early, while others will need additional practice or special support to develop these skills or concepts.

A program without goals and objectives has no foundation. Unstructured presentation of lessons and activities in an unprepared environment is purposeless and may serve to confuse, not inform, children. A solid program for children has thoughtfully developed and regularly modified goals and objectives as its basis.

CONTENT AREAS FOR EARLY CHILDHOOD PROGRAMMING

Content for early childhood programs is generally based on the same discipline areas accepted in the rest of education. These areas, language arts, health and safety, mathematics, science, and social studies, are illustrated in Figure 5–3, Topics and Skills for Units of Study in the Early Childhood Curriculum. These are also the disciplines that provide the knowledge and skills essential to survival in Western culture. Each of these areas is discussed here.

*For the purposes here, *lessons* refers to those experiences that are teacher-led; *activities* refers to those experiences set up by teachers but carried out by children; and *environmental conditions* refers to a specific structuring of materials or equipment designed to facilitate child development.

Language Arts

Language arts study involves facilitation of children's expressive (spoken) and receptive (understood) vocabulary. The early childhood center also seeks to develop listening (necessary for conversation and information gathering), prewriting, and prereading skills. Development of eye-hand coordination, awareness of left-to-right progression, and letter recognition are among those skills that prepare youngsters for the writing and reading activities of the kindergarten and primary grades.

Mathematics and Science

Mathematics and science concepts at the preschool level are primarily dependent on a youngster's level of abstract thinking. Early in development, the child is largely reliant on concrete experiences for understanding. Use of the senses is essential as the child explores materials in order to grasp ideas such as comparison and contrast, classification, and identification of patterns. Most children are unable, however, to comprehend the use of abstract symbols (numbers and letters) until a higher level of cognitive growth has been achieved.

However, many mathematics and science topics and skills can be introduced to preschoolers. Young children can learn to observe, experiment, and predict using their senses in familiar outdoor and indoor environments. They can learn basic facts about plants, animals, weather, magnets, machines, flotation, earth, sky, water, and seasons in the natural sciences. Mathematics concepts may include rote counting, creating sets, temporal relations, seriation, whole-part relations, spatial relations, and measurement skills. Each of these provides part of the essential foundation for learning mathematics operations and science skills in the elementary school.

One of the great controversies of the 1980s involves the validity of teaching mathematics and reading to preschoolers. If one has a basic grasp of the development of eye muscles and coordination, it is apparent that most preschoolers lack the capacity for extensive skills growth in these two areas. Introducing numbers and letters to preschoolers is not inappropriate, and pressure to demonstrate advanced skills at too early an age can have negative impacts on both cognitive and emotional growth.

Social Studies

Social studies at the preschool level has a slightly different focus than that in the elementary school. If one thinks of aspects of the child's world as a series of concentric circles around him or her, the social studies curriculum should begin at the core and work outwards. That is, the child first needs to learn about him- or herself, appearance, sex, ethnic group,* and feelings. Then the family becomes the topic of social studies. At first, the child is discussed in relation to his or her family. Later, the focus shifts to other family members and their roles and work. Finally, the child learns about the community, including his or her school and all those persons and places providing other services to families.

The reason for introducing social studies in this fashion is the child's egocentric nature. Children are most aware of and understand best what concerns them. This together with cognitive restraints such as limited understanding of space and time, explains why the child is not prepared to deal with concepts like people in other nations.

Health and Safety

Health and safety education is yet another component of the early childhood curriculum. An often-neglected aspect of education at this level, this area is of critical and immediate importance to the young child, as information and care for child health education make the difference in a youngster's well-being. It is sometimes assumed by child care and education professionals that the mere provision of a safe and healthy environment is adequate, but it is also important for young children to learn the reasons for and ways of providing a healthy way of life for themselves.

Children can learn during the preschool years about what constitutes a healthy diet, adequate exercise and rest, cleanliness of body, and care of teeth. In addition, information about hazards created by poisonous substances, water, fire, traffic, and strangers can safeguard a young child's life. One of the great benefits of a strong health and safety program is that parents can also benefit from it, and quality of life may be improved for the entire family.

The physical development component is often treated as a separate feature of the curriculum. In actuality, it is a part of the overall health program for children. Emphasis on overall fine- and gross-motor skills and related self-help skills such as dressing and tying shoes not only facilitates a youngster's physical development, but affects the child's self-confidence and self-esteem in a positive way throughout childhood. Youngsters who feel good about their physical skills and can play games, complete crafts and projects, and handle writing and cutting

*Discussion of ethnic groups does not refer to issues like race relations. Rather, children can learn about culturally different foods, music, and customs as these pertain to differences among children who attend the center or program.

implements with ease have a better self-image and are more at ease in attempting new activities.

INDIVIDUALIZING PROGRAMS FOR YOUNG CHILDREN

An important aspect of the program planning process involves consideration of the needs of the individual child as well as of the group. There are a variety of tools useful in the achievement of this aim. For example, child health histories, observations of youngsters, developmental screening instruments, and information from parent-teacher conferences can all be useful (see Section 6). Often, however, the process of identifying individual needs ends with teacher awareness. Specific procedures should be developed for staff in each program to follow so that activities can be modified to truly address the developmental needs of particular youngsters. Sample guidelines are offered in Figure 5–4.

While children can often benefit from group activities in which everyone does similar things, there are other occasions when youngsters can regress or become withdrawn by being pushed beyond their levels of comfort and capability. By contrast, a child who is insufficiently challenged may develop uncooperative or acting-out behaviors in response. Individualizing for children both in one-to-one situations and during group interaction and preparing an environment responsive to unique needs is one of the most important aspects of programming.

Figures 5–5 and 5–6 present general outlines for lesson planning and planning for effective use of instructional materials and equipment with individual children and groups. Figure 5–7, Basic Equipment and Materials List provides a list of items for both infants and toddlers, and preschoolers. Figures 5–8, 5–9, and 5–10 include models for designing floor plans, a list of criteria for a classroom layout, and an integrated curriculum model featuring activities related to the theme "A Trip to the Dentist."

EVALUATION OF CHILDREN'S PROGRAMS

In order to maintain high-quality programs for young children, it is essential to establish systems and timetables for regularly assessing program impact. Not only children's progress, which is affected by many aspects of a youngster's life, but the environment and interpersonal aspects of the program should come under scrutiny. Information should be sought from as many sources as possible, including evaluation instruments and feedback from children, parents, staff, community, and board members. Evaluation should be tied to predetermined criteria, or how the program should ideally function, such as those criteria identified in Figure 5–11.

Evaluation procedures are of no consequence if there is no plan for the information resulting from it. When the results of assessments are known, parties involved should meet to determine how these may best be used to improve the program and benefit participants.

Unfortunately, many administrators and teachers are uncomfortable with evaluation. Preferring to focus only on what appears to work well, they shy away from what they fear will reveal weaknesses in themselves and their programs. There is, however, no shame in seeking improvement. Regular evaluation provides the means for staff and families to see and be part of the process of growth and change.

Figure 5–1

SAMPLE GOALS FOR THE EARLY CHILDHOOD YEARS

Social-Emotional Development

1. To develop positive self-concept
2. To appropriately express both negative and positive feelings
3. To separate from family without serious emotional distress
4. To develop independent behaviors
5. To participate alone and with a group in a variety of experiences
6. To name members and relationships of family
7. To ask for assistance when experiencing difficulty with tasks or relationships
8. To develop acceptable attention-getting behaviors
9. To accept strengths and weaknesses
10. To develop cooperative behaviors for interactions with others
11. To develop relationships with peers and adults outside the home
12. To respect one's own property and that of others
13. To respect individual differences
14. To recognize and respect the feelings and needs of others
15. To develop basic understanding of the history, celebrations, art, music, and other aspects of Western culture

Cognitive Development

1. To point to familiar objects and body parts
2. To name familiar objects and body parts
3. To recognize basic shapes and primary colors
4. To follow simple directions
5. To ask questions
6. To recognize numerals and alphabet letters
7. To classify objects according to common attributes
8. To compare and contrast objects according to predetermined criteria
9. To develop observation skills using the senses
10. To experiment with objects in the environment
11. To predict the outcome of events and experiments
12. To recognize simple patterns
13. To develop basic concepts of space, time, and number
14. To develop problem-solving skills
15. To recall and describe events

Figure 5–1 SAMPLE GOALS FOR THE EARLY CHILDHOOD YEARS (continued)

Language Development

1. To use verbal expression, rather than gestures
2. To develop vocabulary
3. To speak clearly and develop articulation skills
4. To speak in complete sentences
5. To relate experiences
6. To formulate questions
7. To answer (respond to) questions from others
8. To follow simple directions
9. To repeat familiar nursery rhymes, songs, and jokes
10. To listen to stories
11. To retell stories in own words
12. To recognize familiar sounds
13. To participate in writing activities
14. To express ideas, feelings, and experiences through stories and drawings
15. To associate spoken and written language

Physical Development

1. To exhibit age-appropriate balance and coordination skills
2. To safely utilize outdoor equipment for climbing, riding, swinging, etc.
3. To participate in a range of outdoor and indoor physical activities for fine- and gross-motor skills
4. To follow music/drum beat during movement activities
5. To build with various materials (blocks, boxes, etc.), safely employing woodworking equipment as needed
6. To acquire skills for writing, cutting, and eating
7. To handle books comfortably and carefully
8. To dress self and fasten clothing
9. To comfortably experiment with clay, fingerpaint, sand, and other media
10. To participate in a regular program of exercise and physical activity
11. To utilize manipulative toys for nesting, stacking, insertion, matching, and grouping
12. To move comfortably through space without frequent accidents
13. To develop skills for personal hygiene and care (handwashing, toothbrushing, etc.)
14. To handle materials and animals gently
15. To develop confidence in motor-skills abilities

Figure 5–2

SAMPLE OBJECTIVES FOR THE EARLY CHILDHOOD SUBJECT AREAS*

SUBJECT AREA: LANGUAGE ARTS

AGE	*CONCEPT OR SKILL*	*SUBTOPIC*	*OBJECTIVE*
3	Points to picture	Listening	**1.** When shown pictures of familiar objects, the child will be able to give the name of the object (cat, dog, house, cup, etc.).
3	Identify objects when told their use	Listening	**2.** When the use of a familiar object is described, as in, "What do we put our milk in and drink from?" the child will be able to name the object.
3	Gives first and last name	Speaking	**3.** When asked "What is your name?" the child will be able to respond with first and last names.
4	Ask *what* and *where* questions	Speaking	**4.** When asking a question to obtain information, the child will be able to construct a sentence using the words *what* or *where*.
4	Understand size comparatives such as *big* and *bigger*	Listening	**5.** The child will be able to select and present the largest of three blocks, when asked "Bring me the biggest block."
4	Carry out a series of two to four related directions	Listening	**6.** The child will be able to set the table according to directions, when told how to place the plates and silverware at each child's seat.
4	Talk in sentences of three or more words, the sentences taking the form agent-action-object	Speaking	**7.** When asked the question "What color is the cat?" the child will be able to respond with a full sentence, as in, "The cat is black."

*Kathleen Pullan Watkins and Lucius Durant, Jr., "Objectives for the Early Childhood Years Three to Seven," in *Target I*, ed. Marian Giles (Amarillo, TX: Teaching Pathways, Inc., 1983. Reprinted by permission.

Figure 5–2 SAMPLE OBJECTIVES (continued)

AGE	*CONCEPT OR SKILL*	*SUBTOPIC*	*OBJECTIVE*
4	Repeat at least one nursery rhyme and sing a short song	Speaking	**8.** The child will be able to sing or say the rhyme "Itsy, Bitsy Spider" after repeating it with the class several times.
5	Follow three unrelated commands in proper order	Listening	**9.** When given a series of directions for straightening up the classroom, for example, "First, pick up the blocks, then straighten the chairs, and then put the books away," the child will be able to follow all instructions as given.
5	Understand sequence of events when told them	Listening	**10.** When told of an upcoming sequence of events, the child will demonstrate understanding of these by responding correctly to the question "What are we supposed to do next?"
5	Asks *when, how,* and *why* questions	Speaking	**11.** The child will be able to ask for information by using *when, how,* and *why* questions.
5	Talk about causality by using *because* and *so*	Speaking	**12.** When asked for an explanation, the child will be able to give a child-logical response in the form of a sentence that includes the words *because* and *so.*
6	Incorporate verbal directions into play activities	Listening	**13.** Given a set of directions for the use of an interest center, the child will be able to demonstrate understanding of those directions (for example, "Keep all the game pieces on the table").
6	Take appropriate turns during a conversation	Speaking	**14.** During circle activity the child will wait to speak until his or her turn is indicated by the teacher or by the child's turn in line.

Figure 5–2 SAMPLE OBJECTIVES (continued)

AGE	CONCEPT OR SKILL	SUBTOPIC	OBJECTIVE
6	Recognize and say letters in own first and last name	Reading	**15.** When shown various letters of the alphabet and asked "Whose name begins with this letter?" the child will be able to verbally indicate the letter name and own name.
6	Print letters of first name	Writing	**16.** Given a pencil and paper, the child will be able to print the letters of his or her own first name using a model.
7	Understand and observe rules for listening, speaking, and behavior in library, classroom, on playground, etc.	Listening	**17.** On a trip to the library, the child will be able to demonstrate understanding of rules about speaking, tone of voice, etc., by keeping voice low and not disturbing other readers.
7	Repeat a series of events in order of their occurrence	Speaking	**18.** When asked to tell the story of a recent field trip, the child will be able to relate the events of the trip in order of their occurrence.
7	Recognize and say names of familiar objects	Reading	**19.** Shown a series of words that represent familiar objects, the child will be able to name the objects (chair, clock, toy, dog, cat, etc.).
7	Print letters of first and last name accurately	Writing	**20.** Given a pencil and lined paper, the child will be able to print all of the letters of both first and last names accurately.

SUBJECT AREA: MOTOR DEVELOPMENT/GROSS-MOTOR SKILLS

AGE	CONCEPT OR SKILL	OBJECTIVE
3	Run forward	**1.** While playing a game of tag on the playground, the child will be able to run forward to chase or escape another child for a distance of fifteen feet.
3	Jump in place, two feet together	**2.** During a circle game, the child will be able to jump in place with two feet together when asked to "Hop like a rabbit."

Figure 5–2 SAMPLE OBJECTIVES (continued)

AGE	CONCEPT OR SKILL	OBJECTIVE
3	Stand on one foot with assistance	**3.** With an adult holding an arm or elbow, the child will be able to stand on one foot for a period of 5 seconds.
3	Walk on tiptoe	**4.** Following a demonstration by the teacher, the child will be able to walk on tiptoe for a distance of 6 to 10 feet.
3	Kick ball forward	**5.** During an outdoor game of kickball, the child will be able to kick a large ball forward for a distance of 5 feet.
4	Walk on a line	**6.** Given a masking-tape line on the floor of the classroom, the child will be able to walk on the line unassisted for a distance of 6 feet.
4	Balance on one foot for 5 to 10 seconds	**7.** When asked, the child will be able to balance on one foot for a minimum of 5 seconds.
4	Push, pull, steer wheeled toy	**8.** In the gymnasium, the child will be able to operate a child-size wagon with a rider by pushing, pulling, and steering it with a rider.
4	Ride (steer and pedal) tricycle	**9.** Given a tricycle, the child will be able to pedal and steer it for a distance of 20 feet with a minimum of difficulty.
4	Throw overhand, catch ball	**10.** During a game of catch using a large ball, the child will be able to throw the ball overhand and catch the ball 3 out of 5 times.
5	Walk backward toe-to-heel	**11.** Following a demonstration by the teacher, the child will be able to walk backward placing toe to heel for a distance of 5 to 7 feet.
5	Jump forward 10 times without falling	**12.** When asked to imitate a rabbit's hopping motion, the child will be able to jump forward for 10 hops without falling.
5	Walk up and down stairs alone, alternating feet	**13.** Given a flight of at least 4 steps, the child will be able to walk up and down the stairs alternating feet.
5	Turn somersaults	**14.** Given a tumbling mat or grassy outdoor plot, the child will be able to turn at least 3 somersaults without losing balance or falling to the side.

Figure 5–2 SAMPLE OBJECTIVES (continued)

AGE	*CONCEPT OR SKILL*	*OBJECTIVE*
5	Jump rope	**15.** Given an individual jump rope, the child will be able to turn and jump the rope for 2 rope turns.
6	Run lightly on toes	**16.** At a signal from the teacher, the child will be able to run forward on tiptoe for a distance of 10 feet.
6	Walk on balance beam	**17.** The child will be able to walk on a balance beam placed 6 inches off the floor for a distance of 10 feet.
6	Hop up to distance of 6 feet, 6 inches	**18.** The child will be able to hop forward without losing balance for a distance of 6 feet, 6 inches.
6	Skip on alternate feet	**19.** Following the teacher, the child will be able to skip while alternating feet for a distance of 15 feet.
6	Roller-skate	**20.** Given a smooth, unobstructed surface, the child will be able to roller-skate forward for a distance of 10 feet with a minimum of assistance.
7	Ride bicycle well	**21.** Given a smooth, unobstructed surface, the child will be able to ride a bicycle without assistance, maintaining balance and observing safety rules.
7	Throw ball with skill	**22.** Given a softball, the child will be able to toss and catch the ball from a distance of 10 feet.
7	Handle dressing	**23.** The child will be able to handle his or her own dressing completely, including tying shoes and buttoning, zipping, and snapping all clothing.
7	Begin to whistle	**24.** The child will be able to imitate with fair accuracy three whistled notes demonstrated by the teacher.
7	Jump rope skillfully	**25.** The child will be able to jump rope without errors for 5 continuous turns when it is turned by two other children.

Figure 5–2 SAMPLE OBJECTIVES (continued)

SUBJECT AREA: MOTOR DEVELOPMENT/FINE-MOTOR SKILLS

AGE	*CONCEPT OR SKILL*	*OBJECTIVE*
3	String 4 large beads	**1.** Given a medium-weight string with even, unbroken ends, the child will be able to string 4 large beads with holes adequate for the string to pass through.
3	Turn pages singularly	**2.** Given a storybook with six medium-weight pages, the child will be able to turn the pages singularly without tearing them.
3	Snip with scissors	**3.** Given construction paper and scissors appropriate for hand dominance (left or right), the child will be able to manipulate the scissors in an open and closed movement that snips at the paper.
3	Hold crayon with thumb and fingers	**4.** Given a regular-sized, unbroken crayon, the child will be able to approximate the position for holding the crayon using thumb and fingers, after a demonstration by the teacher.
3	Use one hand singularly for most activities	**5.** During activities that require reaching and grasping, the child will be able to demonstrate the ability to use one hand singularly.
4	Build block tower of 6 to 9 blocks	**6.** Given a series of 6 to 9 unit blocks and asked to make a "building" or "house," the child will be able to stack the blocks so they do not fall.
4	Accurately drive pegs into pegboard	**7.** Given 4 medium-sized pegs, a pounding bench, and hammer, the child will be able to accurately drive the pegs into the bench until the peghead is level with the bench.
4	Copy circle shape	**8.** After watching the teacher draw a 2-inch circle, the child will be able to accurately copy a similar-sized and shaped circle using a crayon or pencil.
4	Copy cross-shape	**9.** After watching the teacher draw a cross using two intersecting lines, the child will be able to accurately copy a similarly sized cross using a crayon or pencil.
4	Make clay ball, snake	**10.** Given a lump of clay approximately fist-sized, the child will be able to roll ball and make snake shapes when these are demonstrated by the teacher.

Figure 5–2 SAMPLE OBJECTIVES (continued)

AGE	*CONCEPT OR SKILL*	*OBJECTIVE*
5	Cut on line	**11.** Given scissors appropriate for hand dominance (left or right) and a small sheet of paper with a large, dark line, the child will be able to cut along the line for a distance of 4 inches with fair accuracy.
5	Copy square	**12.** After watching the teacher draw a 2-inch square, the child will be able to accurately copy a similar-sized square using a crayon or pencil.
5	Copy triangle	**13.** After watching the teacher draw a 2-inch triangle, the child will be able to accurately copy a similar-sized triangle using a crayon or pencil.
5	Print a few capital letters	**14.** Given a crayon or pencil and lined paper, the child will be able to print the capital letters of his or her first name using models written by the teacher.
5	Hold pencil with thumb and fingers	**15.** Given a regular-sized pencil, the child will be able to hold the pencil in a position for writing using the thumb and fingers.
6	Cut out large, simple shapes	**16.** Given scissors appropriate for dominance (left or right) and printed shapes two to three inches in diameter, including a circle, square, and triangle, the child will be able to accurately cut out the shapes from the paper.
6	Copy first name	**17.** Given a pencil, lined paper, and a model prepared by the teacher, the child will be able to copy his or her first name accurately.
6	Color within lines	**18.** Given crayons and a simple drawing, the child will be able to color the picture, staying primarily within the lines.*
6	Trace diamond shape	**19.** After watching the teacher trace several 2-inch diamond shapes, the child will be able to accurately trace the shape using a pencil and paper.
6	Print numerals 1 through 10	**20.** Given models of numerals 1 through 10, a pencil, and lined paper, the child will be able to accurately print the numerals with some reversals.

*Please note that while using crayon activities as a measure of fine-motor control and for additional practice, adults should not make an issue of neatness.

Figure 5–2 SAMPLE OBJECTIVES (continued)

AGE	CONCEPT OR SKILL	OBJECTIVE
7	Demonstrates that handedness is well established	**21.** During a series of activities that require reaching and grasping, the child will be able to demonstrate preference for the use of one hand (either left or right).
7	Use simple tools with skill (hammer)	**22.** Given two 12-inch pieces of wood, nails, and hammer, the child will be able to accurately and safely nail the two pieces of wood together.
7	Paste and glue well	**23.** Given materials for making a collage, the child will be able to neatly and accurately paste collage pieces to paper.
7	Print numerals 1 through 15	**24.** Given a pencil and lined paper, the child will be able to accurately print numerals 1 through 15.
7	Use adult pencil grasp	**25.** Given a regular-sized pencil, the child will be able to demonstrate the proper position for writing.

SUBJECT AREA: MATHEMATICS

AGE	CONCEPT OR SKILL	OBJECTIVE
3	Rote counting	**1.** When asked to do so, the child will be able to count aloud up to 5.
3	Recognition of number of objects in a set	**2.** When shown a group of 5 rods, the child will be able to touch each while counting from 1 to 5.
3	Set creation	**3.** Given a set of three cups and one set of three saucers, the child will be able to create three sets of one cup and one saucer each.
3	Whole/part relations	**4.** When asked to give a "piece" of apple to another, the child will be able to separate the fruit and give a single section to the other child.
4	Comparison/ contrast of sets	**5.** When shown two sets of objects, the child will be able to correctly identify the set that has "more" and the set that has "fewer" members.
4	Temporal relations	**6.** The child will be able to correctly respond "yesterday," when asked the question, "When did we go to the library?"

Figure 5–2 SAMPLE OBJECTIVES (continued)

AGE	*CONCEPT OR SKILL*	*OBJECTIVE*
4	Seriation	**7.** Given a series of three rods of different lengths, the child will be able to correctly place them in order from smallest to largest.
4	Recognition of geometric shapes	**8.** The child will be able to point to a round object when asked the question "Show me a circle."
5	Recognition of number names (verbal)	**9.** Given a series of plastic disks, the child will be able to answer the question "How many are there?"
5	Classification	**10.** Given a pile of assorted objects, the child will be able to correctly place the round objects in one pile.
5	Recognition of patterns	**11.** Given a series of blocks in red-blue-red-blue-red pattern, the child will be able to correctly respond "blue" when asked "What comes next?"
5	One-to-one correspondence	**12.** When asked to set the table, the child will correctly place one napkin, cup, plate, fork, and spoon before each plate.
6	Duplication of patterns	**13.** Given a pattern consisting of small cubes of different colors, the child will be able to complete the pattern correctly by adding more blocks.
6	Recognition of number names (auditory)	**14.** When asked the question "Give me five blocks," the child will be able to hand the requestor the correct number.
6	Developing spatial relations	**15.** The child will be able to correctly respond to verbal commands such as "Put the game here and the plate over there."
6	Establishing concepts of time (verbal)	**16.** Using four different wind-up toys the child will observe and be able to describe which toy takes the longest and which the shortest time to unwind.
7	Creating a pattern	**17.** Given a box of colored rods of different sizes and colors, the child will be able to create and duplicate his or her own pattern.
7	Establishing measurement skills	**18.** When observing two children placed back to back, the child will be able to verbally indicate which is taller and which is shorter.
7	Establishing concepts of time (symbolic)	**19.** The child will be able to answer "twelve o'clock" when asked "At what time do we eat lunch?"

Figure 5–2 SAMPLE OBJECTIVES (continued)

AGE	*CONCEPT OR SKILL*	*OBJECTIVE*
7	Conservation	**20.** Given two balls of clay of equal amounts, the child will be able to indicate that these still contain the same amount after one ball has been rolled into a cylindrical shape.

SUBJECT AREA: SCIENCE

AGE	*CONCEPT OR SKILL*	*SUBTOPIC*	*OBJECTIVE*
3	Classification	The senses	**1.** The child will be able to indicate by pointing when asked the question "What part of our bodies do we see with?"
3	Comparison and contrast	Animals	**2.** Given pictures of animals, the child will be able to correctly name the animals that live in our homes.
3	Observation	The senses	**3.** Given a series of similar substances to taste (sugar, flour, salt), the child will be able to correctly identify the substances that taste sweet.
3	Comparison and contrast	Animals	**4.** The child will be able to identify the animals with fur when shown photographs of a fish, a cat, a bear, and a snake.
4	Classification	Plants	**5.** Shown pictures of a variety of plants, the child will be able to place the photographs of those plants with flowers in one group.
4	Observation	Weather	**6.** Following a period of observation, the child will be able to describe the color and condition of the sky (clear, cloudy, sunny).
4	Experimentation	Plants	**7.** The child will be able to participate in an experiment to determine the effects of lack of water and sunlight on plants by taking turns with other children involved in the plant-care process.

Figure 5–2 SAMPLE OBJECTIVES (continued)

AGE	*CONCEPT OR SKILL*	*SUBTOPIC*	*OBJECTIVE*
4	Prediction	Weather	**8.** After an outdoor observation period, the child will be able to describe the weather based on temperature and sky conditions.
5	Record keeping	The human body	**9.** Given a height chart, the child will be able to record his or her growth over a 6-month period and measure the differences using inch-long pieces of colored tape.
5	Classification	Magnets	**10.** Using a magnet, the child will be able to separate a group of objects into those that are metals and those that are not.
5	Comparison	Objects that float	**11.** While experimenting at a water table with objects that float and do not float, the child will be able to list the characteristics of each (light versus heavy).
5	Observation	Seasons	**12.** The child will be able to name the changes characteristic of the season following observation periods.
6	Experimentation	Earth/soil	**13.** The child will experiment with various types of soil and make a list of their properties when weighed, combined with water, etc.
6	Prediction	Rocks	**14.** The child will be able to predict which rocks are heaviest after noting their size, feeling their consistency, and making other observations.
6	Record keeping	Sky	**15.** Working with a parent, the child will keep a record of the appearance of the night sky for 5 days, including appearance and size of the moon, visibility of stars, clouds, etc.

Figure 5–2 SAMPLE OBJECTIVES (continued)

AGE	*CONCEPT OR SKILL*	*SUBTOPIC*	*OBJECTIVE*
6	Measurement	Tools	**16.** Given a group of objects, the child will be able to separate those used for some type of measurement (thermometer, ruler, tape measure) into one group and describe their use.
7	Classification	Machines/ tools	**17.** The child will be able to list some of the tools used by people to lift and move heavy objects, given a list of things to be moved (a wrecked car, new automobiles, a load of bricks, oil in barrels).
7	Observation	Ocean/ bodies of water	**18.** Having viewed a film on ocean life, the child will be able to name some animals that live in oceans.
7	Experimentation	Air	**19.** The child will be able to make a pinwheel and, after taking it outside, describe the effects of the wind on the pinwheel and other objects outside.
7	Prediction	Seasons	**20.** During a discussion about seasonal changes, the child will be able to describe how the clothing and activities of people change from one season to another.

SUBJECT AREA: NUTRITION, HEALTH, AND SAFETY

AGE	*CONCEPT OR SKILL*	*OBJECTIVE*
3	Basic food groups	**1.** Given a variety of foods through a well-planned, prepared, and served menu, the child will taste all foods provided (unless prevented by allergy or handicapping conditions.
3	Basic food groups	**2.** Shown photographs of various foods, the child will be able to classify those foods into the four basic food groups: dairy, meat, fruit/vegetable, and grain.

Figure 5–2 SAMPLE OBJECTIVES (continued)

AGE	*CONCEPT OR SKILL*	*OBJECTIVE*
3	Personal hygiene (toileting)	**3.** When using the toilet, the child will be able to demonstrate procedure for cleansing himself or herself with toilet tissue at completion.
3	Personal hygiene (cleanliness)	**4.** Using soap and paper towels, the child will be able to demonstrate the proper technique for handwashing before and after snacks and meals.
4	Basic food groups	**5.** During mealtimes the child will be able to identify the basic food groups to which each of the foods served belongs.
4	Basic food groups	**6.** When asked "What did you have for dinner last night?" the child will be able to name foods served at home and match those with the basic food groups.
4	Personal hygiene (oral care)	**7.** Following teacher's directions, the child will be able to demonstrate the up-and-down motion and rinsing procedure followed during tooth brushing.
4	Personal hygiene (cleanliness)	**8.** During group discussion or circle time, the child will be able to describe the need for cleansing the body through regular bathing or showering.
5	Basic food groups	**9.** The child will be able to state the foods that should be eaten daily from each of the basic food groups when asked "Which foods should you eat each day?"
5	Nutrition (vitamins and minerals)	**10.** When shown pictures of a variety of foods, the child will be able to list the major vitamins in each related food group.
5	Rest and relaxation	**11.** The child will be able to accept and use the rest periods that are part of the daily schedule in the classroom.
5	Fire safety	**12.** At the sound of the fire alarm, the child will be able to demonstrate the proper procedure for evacuating the building during a fire drill.
6	Nutrition (meal planning)	**13.** Following a chart with printed and pictorial directions, the child will be able to work with a small group to prepare and serve a fruit salad to the rest of the class.

Figure 5–2 SAMPLE OBJECTIVES (continued)

AGE	*CONCEPT OR SKILL*	*OBJECTIVE*
6	Personal and group safety	**14.** The child will be able to demonstrate his awareness/observance of established safety rules when outdoors on class walks (field trips or on the playground).
6	Personal hygiene	**15.** When sneezing or coughing, the child will be able to demonstrate the proper use of a paper tissue or handkerchief.
7	Nutrition (consumer awareness)	**16.** When shown television commercials depicting various foods, the child will be able to identify those advertising nutritious foods and reasons for his or her choices.
7	Nutrition (meal planning and preparation)	**17.** Following directions provided by the teacher, the child will be able to work at home with a parent to select and prepare a nutritious dish to serve to classmates at a potluck luncheon.
7	Personal hygiene (individual and sex differences)	**18.** The child will be able to demonstrate awareness of his or her own sex and the difference between boy and girl classmates by using the appropriate lavatory.
7	Personal hygiene (care of the body)	**19.** The child will be able to name and discuss the various parts of the body and their functions when asked the question "What parts of the body do we use for eating and using food?"

SUBJECT AREA: SOCIAL STUDIES

AGE	*CONCEPT OR SKILL*	*SUBTOPIC*	*OBJECTIVE*
3	Self-understanding (personal characteristics)	Self	**1.** When asked "What do you look like?" the child will be able to describe his or her physical characteristics (eye and hair color, tall or short, etc.).
3	Self-understanding (emotions)	Self	**2.** The child will be able to describe the feelings illustrated when shown a series of pictures depicting various emotions.

Figure 5–2 SAMPLE OBJECTIVES (continued)

AGE	*CONCEPT OR SKILL*	*SUBTOPIC*	*OBJECTIVE*
3	Self-understanding (interests)	Self	**3.** Given a choice of interest centers in the classroom, the child will be able to choose one from among four and work there for a 15-minute period.
3	Self-understanding (characteristics)	Self	**4.** The child will be able to describe his or her skin, hair, eye color, and features and will show pride in appearance.
4	Child in relation to family	Self in relation to others	**5.** The child will be able to name the members and roles of the members of his or her family ("Joyce is my mother").
4	Roles of family	Self in relation to others	**6.** When asked "What jobs/work does your mother do?" the child will be able to list the various roles played by his or her mother inside and outside the home.
4	Child's relationship to peers (communication)	Self in relation to others	**7.** When interested in the play of others in an interest center, the child will be able to verbally request to participate (as in "Can I play?").
4	Child's relationship to peers (respect for others)	Self in relation to others	**8.** When handling or looking at the artwork of another child, the child will handle the project carefully and refrain from criticizing the other's efforts.
5	Group participation (cooperation/sharing)	Self in relation to others	**9.** When participating in a group activity, the child will observe rules established by the teacher for group cooperation and turntaking.
5	Group participation (competition)	Self in relation to others	**10.** When involved in a competitive game, the child will show interest in winning but if he or she does not win will also be able to congratulate the winning child.

Figure 5–2 SAMPLE OBJECTIVES (continued)

AGE	*CONCEPT OR SKILL*	*SUBTOPIC*	*OBJECTIVE*
5	Neighborhood/ community (community-helpers' roles)	Self in relation to others	**11.** The child will be able to list local community helpers and describe their roles when asked "Who helps us get our mail?"
5	Neighborhood/ community (community services)	Self in relation to others	**12.** When asked about the services provided in the local community, the child will be able to list at least five (mail delivery, groceries for sale, trash collection, etc.).
6	History/relationship to other family members	Self in relation to past	**13.** After talking with a parent, the child will be able to give the name of at least one grandparent and tell a short story about that person's life or work.
6	History of own neighborhood or town/city	Self in relation to past	**14.** After a visit to a museum, the child will be able to tell something about the dress, play, or habits of children living in the last century.
6	Geography (of own neighborhood)	Self in relation to land and resources	**15.** Working with other children in the class, the child will be able to make a map of the neighborhood around the school.
6	Geography (natural resources)	Self in relation to land and resources	**16.** After seeing a film about the dangers of polluted air and water, the child will be able to write an experience story discussing the ways people might be more conservative with natural resources.
7	Civics (respect for laws)	Self in relation to others	**17.** After a discussion about laws observed by people in the community, the child will be able to list and discuss the laws or rules observed in the school and classroom and how they benefit children.

Figure 5–2 SAMPLE OBJECTIVES (continued)

AGE	*CONCEPT OR SKILL*	*SUBTOPIC*	*OBJECTIVE*
7	Economics/ consumerism	Careful use of personal resources	**18.** After viewing a series of consumer advertisements designed for television, the child will be able to discuss the message conveyed by each, such as "They want us to buy their toys."
7	Sociology (cooperation on project)	Self in relation to others	**19.** Following a field trip to the zoo, the child will be able to participate with others in completing storybooks that describe their trip.
7	Anthropology (respect for other cultures and ethnic groups)	Self in relation to others	**20.** Following the classroom celebration of Hanukkah, the child will be able to compare and contrast the Jewish holiday with the celebration of Christmas.

Figure 5–3

TOPICS AND SKILLS FOR UNITS OF STUDY IN THE EARLY CHILDHOOD CURRICULUM

I. Language Arts

Listening to stories, poems
Dramatizing stories, poems
Learning finger plays
Listening to music
Learning songs
Making books
Writing experience stories
Making puppets/having puppet shows
Telling stories
Keeping records of class activities
Awareness of different languages
Writing and drawing with pencils and crayons
Letter recognition
Following directions
Developing vocabulary
Associating written with spoken language
Oral expression
Using art media to express feelings
Literature appreciation
Handling, using books
Sequencing of events
Describing objects and people
Participating in conversation
Developing articulation skills
Increasing attention span
Understanding opposites
Understanding figures of speech

II. Health and Safety

Bathing and keeping clean
Rest and exercise
Toileting habits
Using tissues for coughing, sneezing
Care of teeth and gums
Visiting the doctor and dentist
Dressing appropriately for the weather
Food preparation and safety
Basic food groups
Nutritious meals and snacks
Illness and medicines
Growth and aging
Understanding feelings
Emergency procedures
Poisons
Fire safety
Traffic safety
Roles of police and fire personnel
Safety around strangers
Protection from sexual abuse
Dangers of drugs and alcohol abuse
Safety in cars and on buses
Water safety
Understanding warning signs
Farm and home equipment safety

III. Mathematics

Temperature (heat and cold)
Measurement
Numbers (rote counting)
Size
Creating sets and subsets
Temporal concepts (time)

Figure 5–3 TOPICS AND SKILLS FOR UNITS OF STUDY (continued)

III. Mathematics (*Cont.*)

- Numerals (recognizing, copying, ordering)
- Seriation
- Shapes
- How people use numbers (addresses, birthdays, telephone numbers)
- One-to-one correspondence
- Problem solving
- Money
- Spatial relations
- Speed
- The calendar
- Place value
- Recognizing, repeating, and extending patterns
- Classifying and sorting
- Matching sets
- Whole-part relations (fractions)
- Equivalency
- Ordering objects and events
- Charts and graphs
- Number operations
- Chance
- Computer awareness
- Odd and even numbers

IV. Science

- Color
- Properties of water
- Bodies of water
- Electricity
- Rocks and soil
- Magnets
- Seasons
- Plants and trees
- Animals and insects (domestic and wild)
- Stars and planets
- The senses
- Magnification
- Texture
- Sound
- The human body
- Weather, wind, clouds
- Weight and balance
- Construction (tools and simple machines)
- Flotation
- Air
- Fire
- Light
- Location in space
- Energy
- Conservation of natural resources
- Experimenting
- Making predictions
- Observation

V. Social Studies

- Feelings
- Families
- Pets (care of)
- Expressing needs and wants
- Individual physical characteristics
- Likes and dislikes
- People's names
- Respecting individual differences
- Handicapping conditions
- Transportation
- Divorce and separation
- Community helpers
- Art appreciation
- Music appreciation
- Drama appreciation
- Celebrations
- Death
- Clothing people wear

Figure 5–3 TOPICS AND SKILLS FOR UNITS OF STUDY (continued)

V. Social Studies (*Cont.*)

Homes people live in
Food people eat
Jobs people have, tools used in various jobs
Different religious beliefs
Sharing and cooperation
Sources of information (television, radio, books, newspapers)
Friendships
Simple map making
Following rules
Manners/observing social conventions

Figure 5–4

FOUR-PHASE PLAN FOR INDIVIDUALIZING PROGRAMS FOR YOUNG CHILDREN

Identify the skill, concept, or behavior to be developed by the child. Identify a short series of activities designed to reach the stated goal and the order in which the child should be introduced to them. Use the following four-step plan to help the child achieve success.

Phase 1: Conduct a one-to-one, teacher-child lesson to introduce the skill.

Phase 2: Select a second activity and pair the child with another who needs practice or who has mastered the skill. This child-child activity provides repetition or peer tutoring.

Phase 3: Assign the child to an activity designed to build the skill; for example, a special job or classroom chore to be done alone. This related activity provides opportunity for additional practice and builds the child's confidence in his or her ability to be successful at a newly learned skill.

Phase 4: Give the child an opportunity to participate in a skill-related large-group activity. Make certain this is a pressure-free situation. The child will have an opportunity to demonstrate skill mastery and will experience enhanced self-esteem.

Note: With the growth of certain skills, especially those related to socialization, the child may need much more one-to-one and small-group practice before involvement in a large-group activity. If the child fails, reassurance and additional practice should be provided.

Figure 5–5

LESSON PLAN FORMAT

Lesson Topic:	(The name of the lesson.)
Objective:	(The skill or knowledge children will gain as a result of participation in the lesson.)
Number of Children:	(The number of children that should participate in the lesson at any given time.)
Development Level or Age:	
Materials:	
Procedures:	(Step-by-step techniques for carrying out the lesson.)
Outcome:	(A description of how the lesson impacts on children, completed after its conclusion.)
Notes/ Follow Up:	(Suggestions for reinforcing skills or concepts taught in the lesson.)

Figure 5–6

PLAN FOR USE OF MATERIALS/EQUIPMENT

Name and Description of Material or Equipment:	(Title or name of equipment or materials.)
Author/Publisher/Supplier:	(Where product is available.)
Purpose:	(Ways in which equipment/materials may be used with children.)
Number of Children:	(The number of children who can utilize materials/equipment at a given time.)
Instructions:	(How equipment/materials should be utilized; for example, where should equipment/materials be set up? Time of day best for use by children?)
Outcome:	(Successes and failures experienced with equipment/materials. Suggestions for change.)

Figure 5–7

BASIC EQUIPMENT AND MATERIALS LIST

For Infants and Toddlers

- ____ Storage shelves, cubbies, cabinets
- ____ Baby barriers (gates)
- ____ Changing tables
- ____ Rocking chairs
- ____ Low tables with attached seats
- ____ High chairs
- ____ Infant seats
- ____ Cribs
- ____ Baby carriages, strollers
- ____ Wind-up swings
- ____ Walkers
- ____ Humidifiers
- ____ Playpens
- ____ Mirrors
- ____ Plastic dishpans for storage of diapers and supplies
- ____ Baby bottles and liners
- ____ Disposable diapers
- ____ Plastic cups with handles and feeding dishes
- ____ Bottle brush
- ____ Can opener
- ____ Food-storage trays
- ____ Infant potty chairs
- ____ Waterproof pads
- ____ Washcloths
- ____ Wading pool
- ____ Extra infant clothing in various sizes
- ____ Blankets and bedding (crib sheets)
- ____ Bibs
- ____ Pacifiers
- ____ Tissues, toilet paper, paper towels
- ____ Record player, records

Toys

- ____ Musical toys
- ____ Activity boards
- ____ Telephones
- ____ Rings
- ____ Balls
- ____ Inflatable toys
- ____ Pull and push toys
- ____ Stacking and nesting toys
- ____ Bubble preparation and blower
- ____ Books
- ____ Soft or cardboard blocks
- ____ Water toys
- ____ Rattles
- ____ Teething toys
- ____ Washable stuffed toys
- ____ Riding toys
- ____ Soft dolls
- ____ Lightweight empty boxes
- ____ Texture balls
- ____ Surprise boxes

Figure 5–7 BASIC EQUIPMENT AND MATERIALS LIST (continued)

For Preschoolers

- ____ Storage cubbies, shelves, cabinets
- ____ Child-sized tables and chairs
- ____ Easels
- ____ Rugs
- ____ Sand/water table
- ____ Cots
- ____ Mirrors
- ____ Plastic dishpans
- ____ Tissues, toilet paper, paper towels
- ____ Extra children's clothing
- ____ Trashcans and liners
- ____ Plastic trays for food services and play

Library Corner

- ____ Books
- ____ Cushions
- ____ Posters
- ____ Comfortable chairs
- ____ Good lighting

Housekeeping Doll Corner

- ____ Dolls, doll clothes
- ____ Hats, dresses, shirts, ties, shoes, belts, handbags for dress-up
- ____ Sink
- ____ Refrigerator
- ____ Stove
- ____ Table and chairs
- ____ Doll bed
- ____ Telephone
- ____ Play food
- ____ Play money
- ____ Empty food containers
- ____ Dishes (plastic)
- ____ Mirror

Manipulative Toys

- ____ Puzzles
- ____ Attribute blocks
- ____ Lego blocks
- ____ Stringing beads
- ____ Pegboards
- ____ Lincoln Logs
- ____ Lotto
- ____ Dressing frames (for snapping, zipping, buttoning, etc.)

Art Corner

- ____ Pencils
- ____ Paper
- ____ Crayons
- ____ Paints

Figure 5–7 BASIC EQUIPMENT AND MATERIALS LIST (continued)

Art Corner (*Cont.*)

- ____ Paste
- ____ Chalk
- ____ Scissors
- ____ Playdough
- ____ Collage materials
- ____ Paste and glue
- ____ Paintbrushes
- ____ Yarn
- ____ Plasticene clay or colored beeswax

Block Corner

- ____ Unit blocks
- ____ Hollow blocks
- ____ Toy animals, dinosaurs
- ____ Community-helper figures (nonsexist)
- ____ Miniature cars, trucks, traffic signs

Music Corner

- ____ Tape recorder
- ____ Record player, records
- ____ Musical instruments (ethnic and handmade, too)

Science Corner

- ____ Weights and scale
- ____ Magnifying glass
- ____ Thermometer
- ____ Plants
- ____ Animals, food
- ____ Rocks of different colors, sizes
- ____ Leaves
- ____ Pine cones
- ____ Bird's nest
- ____ Shells
- ____ Magnets

Large-Muscle Equipment

- ____ Balance beam
- ____ Swings
- ____ Climber
- ____ Wheeled toys
- ____ Push and pull toys
- ____ Jump ropes
- ____ Wading pool
- ____ Tunnels
- ____ Empty boxes
- ____ Slide
- ____ Balls

Miscellaneous

- ____ Puppets, puppet theater
- ____ Water and sand toys

Figure 5–8

MODELS FOR DESIGNING FLOOR PLANS

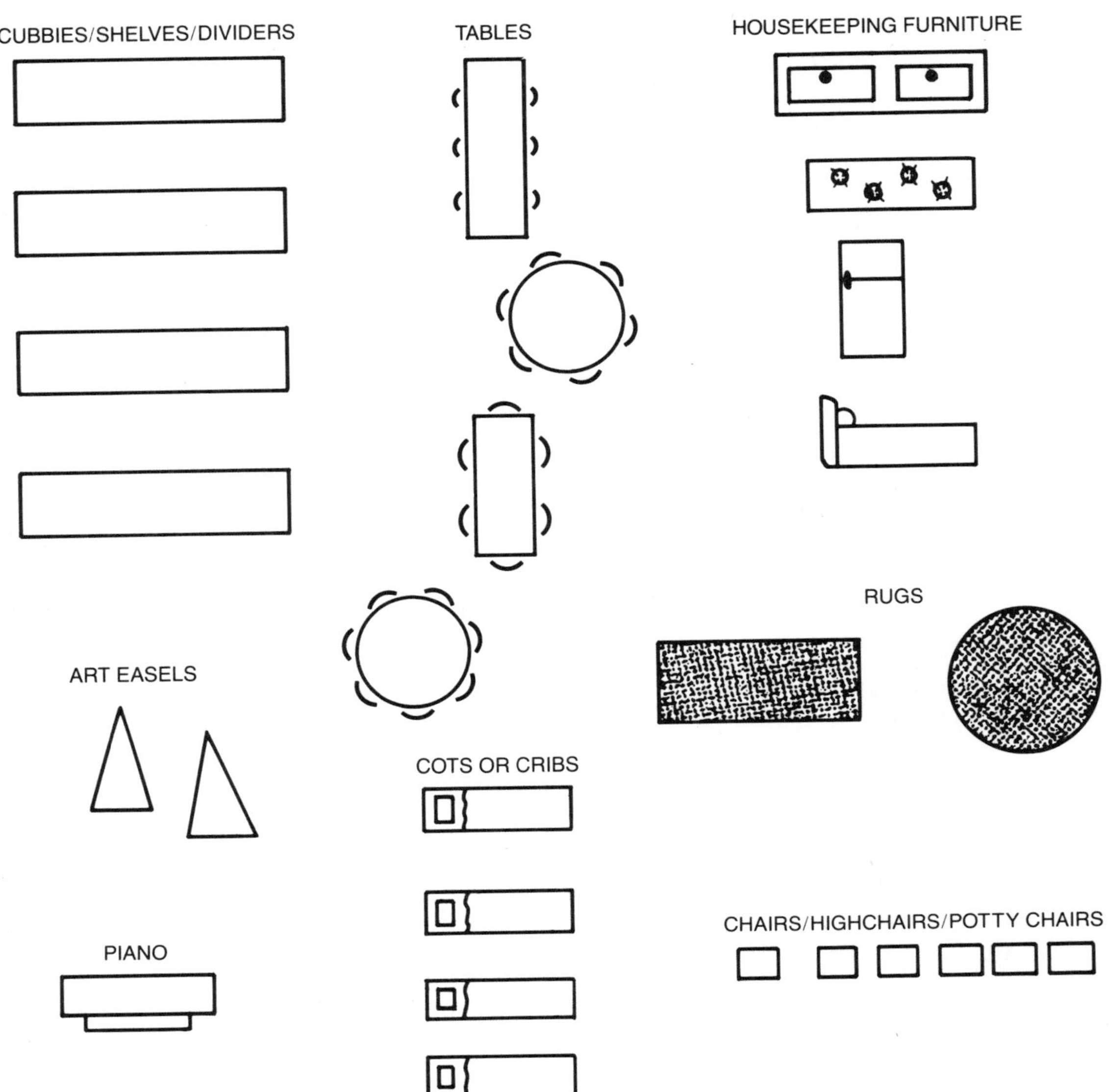

DIRECTIONS: CUT OUT PIECES ABOVE AND ARRANGE AS DESIRED ON THE BLANK FLOOR PLAN PROVIDED.

Figure 5–8 MODELS FOR DESIGNING FLOOR PLANS (continued)

FLOOR PLAN

Figure 5–9

CHECKLIST OF CRITERIA FOR CLASSROOM LAYOUT

	Yes	Improvement Needed	No
I. Developmental Needs of Children			
A. Children have access to available materials			
B. Interest centers have adequate space for several children to play simultaneously			
C. Children have privacy if desired			
D. Children can play in interest centers with a minimum of interference from those engaged in other activities			
E. Storage areas are clearly identified and labeled for easy replacement of materials and cleanup by children			
F. Similar activities (blocks, dramatic play) are close together so they may be combined			
G. Reading and art areas have adequate lighting and are near essential supplies, i.e., art area is near water			
H. Reading and manipulative-toy areas have adequate seating			
I. Interest centers are easily accessible without crossing other areas			
J. Children's work is displayed at their eye level			
K. The number of children permitted in an interest center is indicated using a symbol they know			

Figure 5–9 CHECKLIST OF CRITERIA FOR CLASSROOM LAYOUT (continued)

	Yes	Improvement Needed	No
II. Supervision/Classroom Management Issues for Staff A. Large open spaces which encourage running are avoided			
B. Quiet and noisy areas are separated to limit stress, overstimulation, and conflicts			
C. Areas to store, display children's work are conveniently provided			
D. Emergency and other exits are clear at all times			
E. Teacher/caregiver views of children are not blocked by furniture or equipment			
F. Materials are stored so that interest centers can easily be restocked during the day			
G. Children can use most equipment/materials with a minimum of adult assistance			
H. Equipment/materials can easily be moved when necessary			
I. Teacher/caregiver supplies are out of children's reach			
J. Space is available for individual, small-group, and large-group activities			

Figure 5–10

INTEGRATED CURRICULUM MODEL

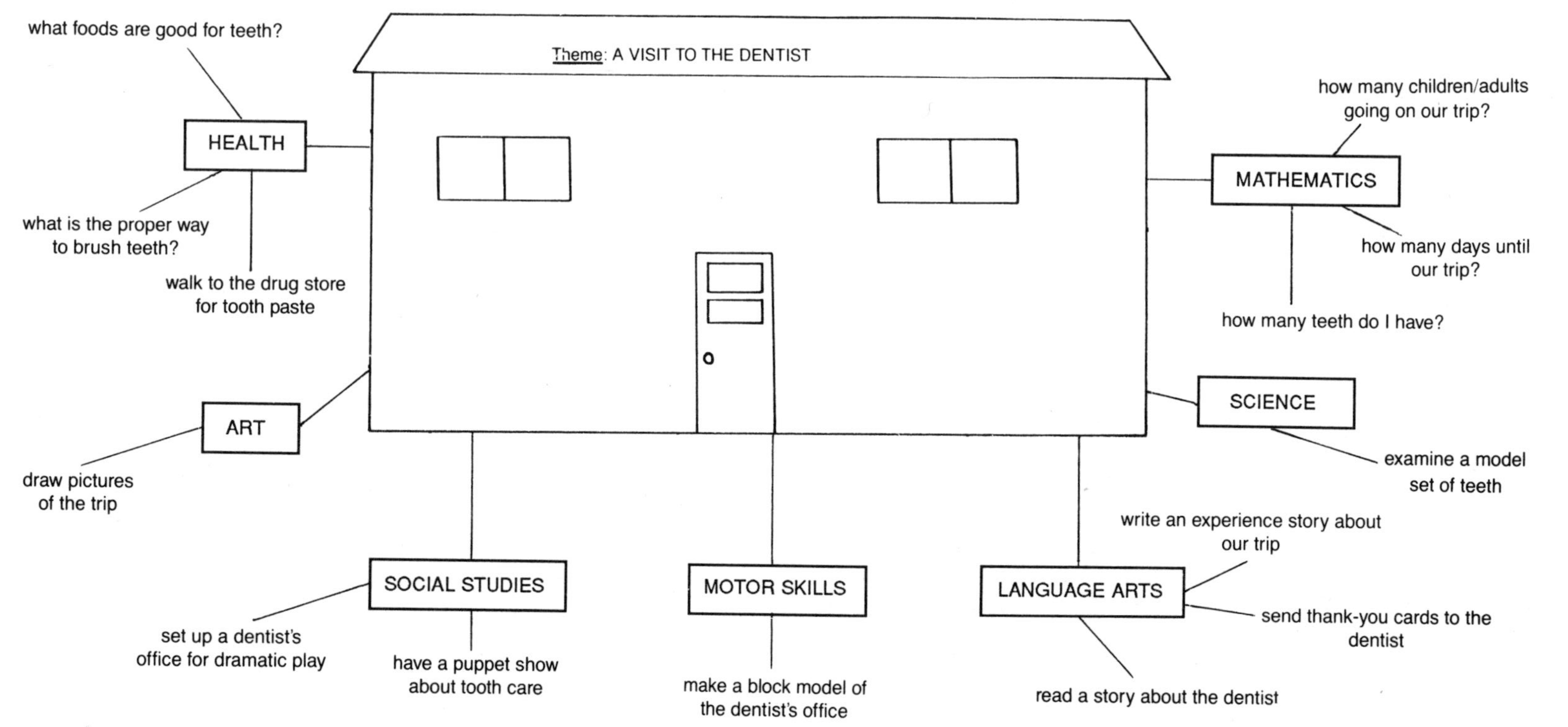

Figure 5–11

CRITERIA FOR EVALUATING CHILDREN'S PROGRAMS*

	Yes	Improvement Needed	No
I. Curriculum Content			
A. A variety of subject areas (mathematics, science, language arts, social studies, health and safety) are visible in daily activities			
B. Children's participation in activities is based on individual needs as determined by teacher observation, child's own choice, etc.			
C. There is a visible and logical sequence to the curriculum			
D. Follow-up activities are provided for all lessons taught			
E. The development of the whole child (physical, cognitive, psychosocial) is facilitated by the curriculum			
F. Curriculum is based on children's previous knowledge, interests, and past experiences			
G. The learning process rather than the products of activities is emphasized			
H. Curriculum is clearly related to program goals and objectives			
I. Curriculum is appropriate for the developmental needs of children served			
J. Children's needs for rest, food, exercise, and elimination are met as a part of the day's activities			

*Reprinted by permission of Philadelphia Parent-Child Center.

	Yes	Improvement Needed	No
K. Important events and aspects of child and family life are integrated into the curriculum			
L. Feedback from parents, volunteers, and community is considered when curriculum is evaluated and modified			
M. Rewards are built into children's activities or are regularly provided by the teacher			
N. Curriculum clearly prepares children to realize success in other settings (elementary school, peer and family interactions)			
II. Teaching Methods A. Written plans for daily activities are available			
B. Individualized, small-group, and large-group activities are regularly conducted			
C. There is a balance between active and quiet activities			
D. The daily schedule is flexible when need is indicated			
E. A balance exists between teacher-led and child-initiated activities			
F. Teacher-facilitation of children's free-choice activities is evident			
G. Teachers deviate from planned procedures when children's needs indicate			
H. Discussion, hands-on experiences, and a broad range of other teaching techniques are regularly employed			
I. Children are urged to take their time and complete projects they are involved in. There are no rigid timetables			

	Yes	Improvement Needed	No
J. Children appear to be familiar with a daily routine			
K. Guidelines for children's behavior are evident and are consistently applied			
L. Children are regularly offered a range of means for expressing ideas, needs, feelings, and demonstrating new acquired skills			
M. Lessons include clearly observable opening and closure			
N. Goals for children are clear to observers and children themselves; there are no hidden agendas			
III. Interpersonal Communications and Atmosphere A. Adults* address children by name and at eye level			
B. Children's activities and behavior appear to be spontaneous and natural			
C. Children express needs and feelings freely			
D. Children's aggressive behavior is limited			
E. Children demonstrate care of the environment, equipment, and materials			
F. Children demonstrate care of own and others' possessions			
G. Adults respond with active listening to children's conversation			
H. Adults seem to enjoy interactions with children			
I. Sharing and cooperation are evidenced by both children and adults			

*Teachers, caregivers, volunteers, etc.

Figure 5–11 CRITERIA FOR EVALUATING CHILDREN'S PROGRAMS (continued)

	Yes	Improvement Needed	No
J. Children continue to behave without supervision in the same ways as they do when teacher(s) is present			
K. Children ask for and receive help with projects or activities			
L. Children share accomplishments with adults and are praised for accomplishments			
M. Adults consult one another and work together smoothly to meet children's needs			
N. Adults permit children to resolve their own problems without interference in most situations			

Further Reading

BAYLESS, K.M., and M.E. RAMSEY. *Music: A Way of Life for the Young Child.* St. Louis: C.V. Mosby, 1978.

COMER, D. *Developing Safety Skills with the Young Child.* Albany, NY: Delmar Publishers, 1987.

COODY, B. *Using Literature with Young Children.* Dubuque, IA: Wm. C. Brown, 1983.

COPPLE, C., et al. *Educating the Young Thinker.* New York: Van Nostrand, 1979.

ELISON, C.F. and L.J. JENKINS. *A Practical Guide to Early Childhood Curriculum.* St. Louis: C.V. Mosby, 1977.

HARLAN, J.D. *Science Experiences for the Early Childhood Years,* 4th ed. Columbus, OH: Merrill, 1988.

HENDRICK, J. *Total Learning: Curriculum for the Young Child,* 2nd ed. Columbus, OH: Merrill, 1986.

KAMII, C. *Number in Preschool and Kindergarten: Educational Implementation of Piaget's Theory.* Washington, DC: National Association for the Education of Young Children, 1982.

LEAVITT, R.L., and B.K. Eheart. *Toddler Day Care: A Guide to Responsive Caregiving.* Lexington, MA: Lexington Books, 1985.

MAXIM, G.W. *The Sourcebook: Activities to Enrich Programs for Infants and Young Children.* Belmont, CA: Wadsworth, 1981.

MONTESSORI, M. *Dr. Montessori's Own Handbook.* New York: Schocken Books, 1965.

MORRISON, G.G. *Early Childhood Education Today,* 4th ed. Columbus, OH: Merrill, 1987.

MORRISON, G.S. *The Education and Development of Infants, Toddlers, and Preschoolers.* Glenview, IL: Scott, Foresman/Little, Brown, 1988.

NEWMAN, D. *The Early Childhood Teacher's Almanac: Activities for Every Month of the Year.* West Nyack, NY: The Center for Applied Research in Education, 1984.

RAMSEY, P.G. *Teaching and Learning in a Diverse World: Multi-Cultural Education for Young Children.* New York: Teachers College Press, 1986.

SEEFELDT, C., ed. *The Early Childhood Curriculum.* New York: Teachers College Press, 1986.

SPODEK, B., et al. *Foundations of Early Childhood Education: Teaching Three-, Four-, and Five-Year Old Children*. Englewood Cliffs, NJ: Prentice Hall, 1987.

WHITE, B.L. *Educating the Infant and Toddler*. Lexington, MA: Lexington Books, 1987.

WILSON, L.C. *Infants and Toddlers: Curriculum and Teaching*. Albany, NY: Delmar Publishers, 1986.

section 6

CHILD & FAMILY INVOLVEMENT IN EARLY CHILDHOOD PROGRAMS

A child's enrollment and participation in a preschool or day care program is, or should be, a family affair. This section provides forms and examples covering different aspects of family involvement in the program.

ENROLLMENT

Parents receive their first impressions of a program when they scrutinize a center during the selection process. Most administrators extend themselves during the recruitment process because they hope families will choose their agencies. However, the most important impression of a program is undoubtedly given at the time of enrollment. It is then that the parents get a picture of the center's depth of interest in their child and in their family as a whole. The parents may also see in detail the potential, or lack of it, for family involvement at the center. For these reasons, we believe that the person selected to conduct intake interviews should be an individual with excellent communication skills, extensive knowledge of the program, and a vested interest in parental participation.

Similarly, when a child is enrolled in a program, the staff has the opportunity to collect an extensive body of information about the youngster and his or her family. While a program should never be intrusive, questions should be asked about the child's birth, development history, family interactions, immunizations, and even eating, sleeping, and elimination habits. An interviewer should seek to display interest in and concern for the family, while avoiding questions that might be mistaken for prying.

Figures 6–1 and 6–2 provide a sample application for a day care program and a detailed developmental history form that can be used as is or adapted to your needs. A card with emergency information, as shown in Figure 6–3, should also be maintained for each child. The Parental Involvement Questionnaire in Figure 6–4 elicits information regarding the parent-child relationship.

At the time of enrollment, the center's policies (see Section 1) along with the responsibilities parents will incur in connection with the child's participation in the program should be made clear to parents. These responsibilities might include requirements for children's clothing and meals, the fee schedule, and other important information.

Although some programs, like Head Start, mandate a degree of parental involvement, parents should feel that they have some choices in the manner of their participation. The enrollment interviewer should seek to identify the interests and talents of adults in the family, their work schedules, and those times when they may be free to volunteer. While volunteerism may be required in some centers, parents should be enticed rather than coerced to participate.

WELCOMING PARENTS

As parents are advised of a program's need for their involvement, it is essential for staff to have a welcoming and positive attitude toward the presence of families at the center. There is no doubt that instituting a parental involvement component is hard work. Finding appropriate ways for parents to participate and contribute to a program takes time and effort even when a program is established, and administrators and teachers need to take time to seek out and evaluate feedback from parents. A variety of possible parental-involvement activities are listed in Figure 6–5.

The attitude of the staff is vital to the success of parental involvement. When staff members understand the value of family participation in the program, they tend to extend themselves to parents, utilizing them at every opportunity. The results are obvious: There are extra pairs of hands to provide children with more one-on-one attention; parents grow in their knowledge about and confidence in their ability to care for their children; and they learn early in the lives of their children the value of their contributions to the educational process. Teachers, on the other hand, have first-hand opportunities to observe the relationship between specific parent-child dyads.

When the staff does not welcome parents, the work of teachers becomes difficult. They must find alternative ways to learn how the child's development is affected by the home environment. Sadly, lack of parental involvement may also erode the confidence of the parents. This happens when mothers and fathers are denied the opportunity to learn about child development and education. The child will grow and learn from participation in the program, but will be denied the support provided when home and school work closely together.

Staff members need to closely examine their attitudes toward parents and, if necessary, work together with them to improve these attitudes through discussion and a gradual immersion in involvement activities. The staff must realize the teacher's role as a link between parent and child, and as an advocate for the family as a whole. The survey in Figure 6–6 can help staff members in their self-assessment.

OBSERVING THE CHILD IN THE DAY CARE CENTER

Many programs care for large numbers of children and have extensive waiting lists. Caring for a group of children in a center or family day care home is time-consuming, and assessing and responding to the needs of the individual child can be difficult. Nonetheless, it is important for teachers and caregivers to be aware of and utilize a variety of means to study the individual child.

Beginning either at the time of enrollment or at the outset of the school year, usually in September, children should receive the first of a series of developmental evaluations. These standardized tools are easy to obtain. Many publishers of early childhood education texts and materials also publish instruments designed to evaluate the developmental level of the individual child. Some instruments are, however, more comprehensive than others. A child-development program should attempt to assess the child's level of growth in areas such as fine- and gross-motor, language, cognitive, social-emotional and self-help skills. This assessment should take place on a regular basis, and at least twice within a twelve-month period. It is crucial during early childhood that developmental problems be identified and responded to. This is the primary reason for a structured, regular assessment of each child's growth.

Figure 6–7 lists ten widely used developmental screening instruments along with a brief description of each and the name and address of the publisher. One of these instruments, the Denver Developmental Screening Test, is illustrated in Figure 6–8.

Staff in early childhood programs should also use less formal means for recording information about children. Checklists, and running and anecdotal records such as those illustrated in Figures 6–9 and 6–10 are some of the ways to document a child's behavior. Among the purposes for observation and record keeping are understanding the situations that produce certain behaviors and changing those behaviors. Usually the behaviors we wish to change are inappropriate or undesirable ones. A child may be disruptive or may be withdrawn and unable to interact with other children, for example. An observation or series of observations can help a teacher or caregiver understand the mechanisms that underline the child's behavior, enabling the teacher or caregiver to formulate a plan to help.

Documentation of other types of problems, such as accident or injury, is also important in the early childhood setting. Figure 6–11 presents a sample form for reporting an accident or illness on the part of a child, staff member, or visitor.

PARENT-TEACHER CONFERENCES

As the staff learns more about a child through parental involvement and through observing and working with the youngsters, it becomes important for parents and teacher to have a formalized exchange of information. Usually this occurs in parent-teacher conferences. Ideally, these should be private meetings conducted at a time when neither party feels rushed or stressed. Parent-teacher conferences should be pleasant exchanges between adults who care about a child. Teachers who only ask for a meeting with a parent when a problem arises convey a very negative message to families—that what is noticed and of consequence is the child's inappropriate behavior. The parents may also feel that their competence is being judged or attacked by the teacher, who represents child-development expertise.

Parent-teacher conferences should be used to support parenting skills and the parent-child relationship. They provide unique opportunities for parents and teacher to exchange anecdotes about the child; for the teacher-caregiver to explain the program; for the parents to update the teacher on what is going on at home. Information shared at these times should be treated as privileged and with utmost discretion.

This section concludes with three forms related to parent-teacher conferences. These include a list of twenty-two suggestions for parent conferences (Figure 6–13), a follow-up conference report (Figure 6–14) that confirms understandings reached during a meeting, and a report on parent conference form (Figure 6–15).

FAMILY CENTERS

Early childhood programs have rapidly developed into centers for families. No longer are they concerned only with the child, but also with how he or she is affected by and affects the family. The importance of the center's input and involvement with families during the earliest child-rearing years is becoming clear, as is the realization that children participate in early childhood programs for only a few years. When these programs help prepare both child and parents for the future, the job is one well done.

Figure 6–1

APPLICATION FOR DAY CARE
GRANT DAY CARE ASSOCIATION

The purpose of securing this information is to help the Day Care staff better understand your child and to help you know what to expect from the Day Care Center or Day Care Home Program. Your child's care during the day is a responsibility we share.

Last Name ______________ Mother ________ Father ________

Address ____________ Telephone No. ________ Marital Status ____

Children (for whom placement is requested):

	NAME	*BIRTHDATE DAY/MO./YEAR*	*PLACE OF BIRTH CITY, STATE, ZIP*	*CENTER (GROUP OR DAY CARE HOME)*
1.				
2.				
3.				
4.				
5.				

Mother's Employer ______________________________

Address ______________________ Telephone No. ________

Work Hours ____________ to ____________ No. of Days ________

Father's Employer ______________________________

Address ______________________ Telephone No. ________

Work Hours ____________ to ____________ No. of Days ________

Figure 6–1 APPLICATION FOR DAY CARE (continued)

Who Will Call for Child (relationship) ______________________

Means of Transportation? ______________________

Other Members of Household (including children not under care)

1. ______________________

2. ______________________

Has the child had previous Day Care Placement? ________

Where? ______________________

Reason for Requesting Placement ______________________

Age of Child Placed in Day Care ______________________

Doctor or Clinic Used ______________________

Address ______________________ Telephone No. ________

Income ____________ Gross (Wkly, Biwkly, Monthly) ________

Other (AFDC, etc.) ____________ No. Days Employed/Week ________

Mother ____________ ____________ ____________

Father ____________ ____________ ____________

Assigned: Social Worker ____________ Facility to Be Used ________

Date to Enter ________ Fee ________ Plan of Payment ________

Insurance ____________ Plan of Payment ____________

Figure 6–2

DEVELOPMENTAL HISTORY

Child's Name ______________________ Birthdate ________
Last First Day/Mo./Yr.

Describe your child briefly (physical appearance, personality, abilities) ________

____

If school-age: Grade placement __________

School's name and location ______________________

____

ADDITIONAL INFORMATION FOR INFANTS AND TODDLERS

Any history of colic? __________

Is baby's skin highly sensitive? ______________________

Frequent diaper rash? ________

Do you use: Oil? ______ Powder? ______ Lotion? ______ Other? ______

Are plastic pants used? Always ______ Sometimes ______ Never ______

Describe child's typical daily schedule ______________________

____

____

Length of time this schedule in use ______________________

Have records of feeding been kept? ______________________

Any special feeding problems? ______________________

Does your child eat unassisted? ______________________

Does he/she enjoy eating? ______________________

How has child been fed? Held in lap ______ Highchair ______ Other ______

Are bowel movements regular? ________ How many per day? ________

What time? ______________

How frequently do accidents occur? ______________________

Is diarrhea __________ or constipation __________ a problem? ________

Does child use a pacifier or suck thumb? __________

Does child pull self to standing position? __________

Crawl? ________________ Walk with support? ________________

Figure 6–2 DEVELOPMENTAL HISTORY (continued)

Does child have a "fussy" time? ________ When? ____________________

How handled ____

____

Has toilet training been attempted? ______ What is used at home? ______

Potty chair? ______ Special toilet seat? ______ Regular toilet seat? ______

Date placement is desired ________________ Fee set ________________

SLEEPING

What time does child go to bed? ____________ Awaken? ____________

When is he/she ready for sleep? ____ Does he/she have own room? ____

Own bed? __________ Does he/she walk, talk, or cry at night? __________

What does he/she take to bed with him/her? ____________________

What is his/her mood on awakening? ____________________

Does he/she take naps? ______ From when ________ To when ________

SOCIAL RELATIONSHIPS

Has he/she had experience playing with other children? ____________

By nature is he/she friendly? __ Aggressive? __ Shy? __ Withdrawn? __

Hoe does he/she get along with brothers and sisters? ____________

Other adults? ______________________________

With what age child does he/she prefer to play? ____________________

Is he/she known by any children in the Center or Day Care Home? ______

Does he/she appear to enjoy being alone? ____________________

How does he/she relate to strangers? ____________________

Does he/she demand a lot of adult attention? ____________________

What makes him/her upset? ____________________________

How does he/she show feelings? ____________________________

What methods do you use when he/she behaves in a way that you do not approve of?

____

Who does most of the disciplining? ____________________________

What frightens your child? ____________________________

Animals? ______________________ People? ______________________

Rough children? ________ Loud noises? ________ Darkness? ________

Storms? ____________________ Anything else? ____________________

Favorite toys and activities at home ______________________________

Does he/she like to be read to? __________ Listen to music? __________

Does he/she prefer to play outdoors? ______________________________

Can he/she ride a tricycle? ______________________________

List child's favorite activities ______________________________

COMMENTS:

In what particular ways can we help your child this year? __________

____

____

____

____

____

Figure 6–3

FAMILY CARD

Name of Family ______________________________
Last First (Mother) First (Father)

CHILDREN UNDER CARE

	LAST NAME	FIRST NAME	BIRTHDAY DAY/MO./YEAR	FACILITY OR GROUP
1.				
2.				
3.				
4.				
5.				

EMERGENCY INFORMATION

Home Address ____________ Home Telephone ____________

Mother's Work Telephone ____________ Hours ____________

Father's Work Telephone ____________ Hours ____________

Emergency Contact*____________ Telephone No. ____________
Last First

*Name of person who has parents' permission to care for child in an emergency

Written permission on file to give care in an emergency?

Yes ____________ No ____________

Date of last tetanus shot? ____________

List allergies ____________

Doctor or Hospital ____________
Name Address

Telephone No. ____________

List all regular medication taken ____________

List health insurance information ____________

Subscriber's Name ____________

Name of insurance ____________

Identification no. ____________

Figure 6–4

PARENTAL INVOLVEMENT QUESTIONNAIRE

Please indicate your agreement or disagreement with each statement in the spaces provided below by marking a "Y" indicating "yes" or "N" indicating "no." Your responses will serve as a tool to determine the similarity of our expectations.

Children must:

__________ Eat all their vegetables before they can have dessert

__________ Answer to their given names rather than nicknames

__________ Share toys they bring from home

__________ Be toilet trained before age two

__________ Not use other children's toothbrushes if they lose theirs

__________ Play outside daily, despite their desires (weather permitting)

__________ Learn to accept authority from adults without argument

Provider should:

__________ Never spank children

__________ Never allow children to be unsupervised

__________ Be consistent when dealing with children

__________ Recognize and consider individual differences among children

__________ Talk with parents freely about their children

__________ Provide choices of activities for children at all times

__________ Allow children to make up their own games and activities

As a parent I would like my child to:

__________ Use good table manners

__________ Be considerate of the needs of others

__________ Be taught to read and write as quickly as possible

__________ Use caution in asking a lot of questions

__________ Be free to explore his/her body and learn to think of it as nice and under his/her personal control

__________ Feel self-confident and good about him/herself

__________ Eat all the food he/she asks for

__________ Stay neat and clean

Figure 6–5

PARENTAL INVOLVEMENT ACTIVITIES

1. Assisting with computer games
2. Assisting at learning centers
3. Reading to children
4. Telling stories
5. Playing instructional games with children
6. Tutoring
7. Helping prepare for holiday/birthday parties
8. Planning workshops for parents
9. Repairing equipment
10. Preparing parent bulletin boards
11. Collecting materials for children's projects
12. Serving as telephone chairperson
13. Contributing to center newsletter
14. Serving as volunteer coordinator
15. Making games and toys
16. Collecting recyclable materials
17. Speaking at parent programs
18. Furnishing dress-up clothes and costumes
19. Making art aprons/smocks
20. Laundering aprons/smocks
21. Donating books to center
22. Accompanying children on field trips
23. Helping to select library books for children
24. Making books, such as a book about shapes or one about colors
25. Sharing hobbies/special talents
26. Working with individual children under teacher's supervision

Add your own suggestions to this partial list.

Figure 6–6

SURVEY OF STAFF ATTITUDES TOWARD PARENTAL INVOLVEMENT

This questionnaire can assist caregivers in assessing their feelings about parental collaboration. It is suggested that the questionnaire be given to staff prior to a regularly scheduled staff meeting and be used as a main topic of discussion.

	Yes	No
1. I find it difficult to work with parents		
2. I have found parents to be an important resource		
3. I find that today's parents are too busy to participate in child-care activities		
4. I enjoy working with parents		
5. I am ill at ease when parents enter my room		
6. I believe that some parents do not care about their children		
7. I openly encourage parents to participate in class activities		
8. I distance myself socially from parents		
9. I feel relieved when all parents have left my room		
10. I feel intimidated by parents		
11. I feel educationally superior to parents		
12. I practice *making eye contact* when talking with parents		
13. I look forward with pleasure to parent conferences		
14. I believe that a close working relationship with parents is important for maximum student growth		
15. I communicate with parents when a child does well as well as when he/she doesn't		
16. I plan activities around goals parents have for their child		
17. I solicit parent volunteers to assist in my room		
18. I send parents examples of their child's work		
19. I believe that many parents send their children to school dressed inappropriately.		

Figure 6–7

DEVELOPMENTAL SCREENING INSTRUMENTS

TEST NAME	*DESCRIPTION*	*TEST PUBLISHER*
The Cattell Infant Intelligence Scale	An individually administered test designed to measure the cognitive development of children from one to thirty months	The Psychological Corporation 757 Third Avenue New York, NY 10017
The Full Range Picture Vocabulary Test	Designed to measure receptive vocabulary, this individually administered test may be used to assess persons as young as two years	Psychological Test Specialists Box 1441 Missoula, MT 59801
The McCarthy Scales of Children's Abilities	Assesses children's general cognitive level along with skills in these areas: verbal, perceptual performance, quantitative, memory and motor. May be individually administered to children between thirty months and eight years	The Psychological Corporation 757 Third Avenue New York, NY 10017
The Peabody Picture Vocabulary Test	Measures intelligence via assessment of receptive vocabulary. Individually administered to persons aged two years and older	American Guidance Service Publisher's Building Circle Pines, MN 55014
Pictorial Test of Intelligence	Assesses intelligence of children three to eight years in seven areas: picture vocabulary, form discrimination, information and comprehension, similarities, size and number, immediate recall, and total performance. Individually administered	Houghton-Mifflin Company The Editor's Offices P.O. Box 1970 Iowa City, IA 52240
The Wechsler Preschool and Primary Scale of Intelligence	Ten subtests measure the intelligence of children aged four to six-and-one-half years. Individually administered	The Psychological Corporation 757 Third Avenue New York, NY 10017

Figure 6–7 DEVELOPMENTAL SCREENING INSTRUMENTS (continued)

The Bayley Scales of Infant Development	Measures the mental and psychomotor development of children two to thirty months. Individually administered	The Psychological Corporation 757 Third Avenue New York, NY 10017
The Psycho-Educational Evaluation of the Preschool Child	Designed to be used in conjunction with other standardized tests. Assesses development in the areas of physical and sensory growth, perception, memory, language, and cognition. Allows teacher to design teaching prescriptions	Greene & Stratton, Inc. 111 Fifth Avenue New York, NY 10003
The Denver Developmental Screening Test	An individually administered test that helps to identify children at risk for developmental delay and behavioral problems. Administered to children from one month to six years of age	Ladoca Project & Publishing Company East 51st Avenue and Lincoln Street Denver, CO 80216
The Gessell Developmental Schedules	Individually assesses the developmental status of children one month to six years of age in the areas of motor, adaptive, language, and personal skills	The Psychological Corporation 757 Third Avenue New York, NY 10017

Figure 6–8

SAMPLE SCREENING INSTRUMENT

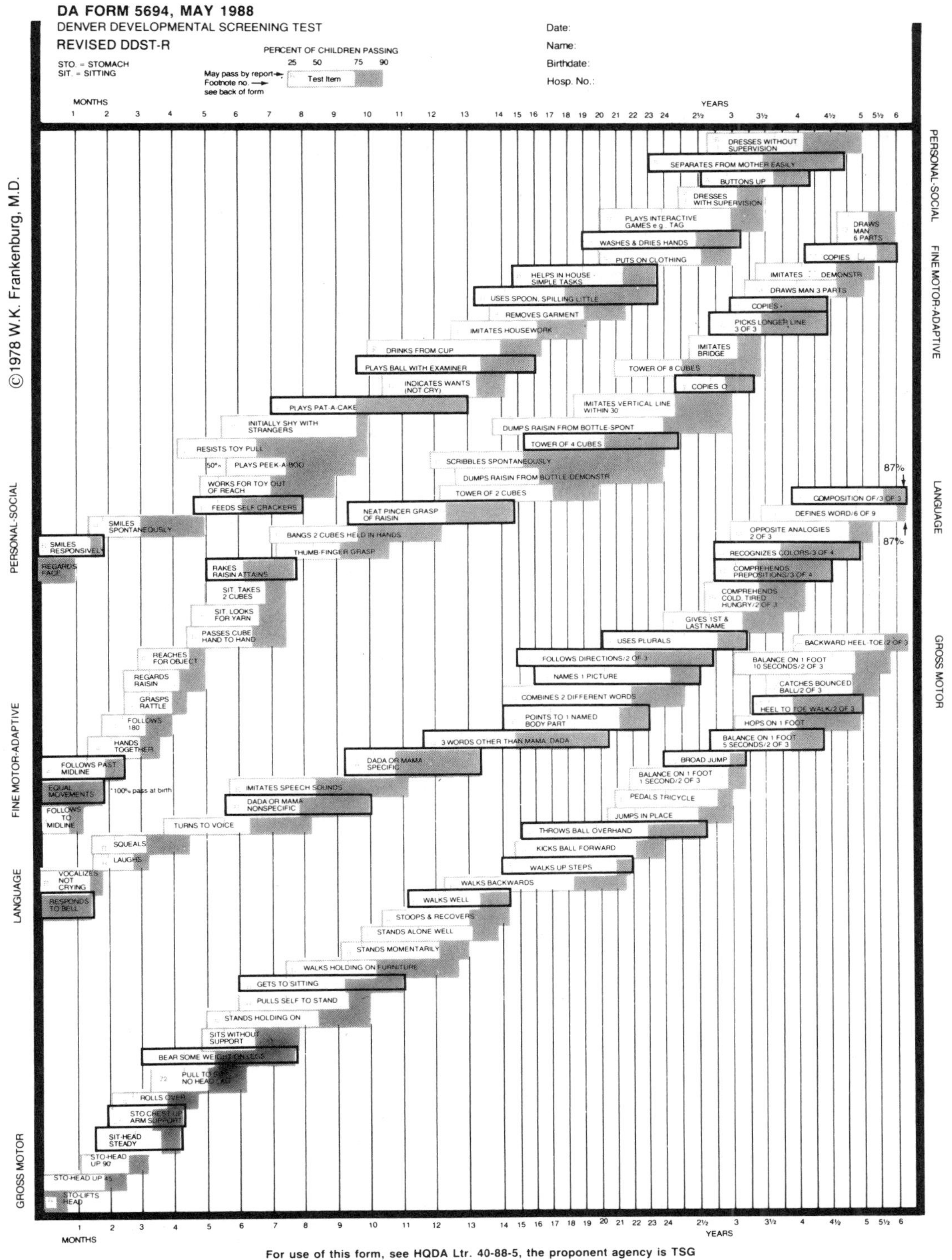

For use of this form, see HQDA Ltr. 40-88-5, the proponent agency is TSG

Figure 6–8 SAMPLE SCREENING INSTRUMENT (continued)

1. Try to get child to smile by smiling, talking or waving to him. Do not touch him.
2. When child is playing with toy, pull it away from him. Pass if he resists.
3. Child does not have to be able to tie shoes or button in the back.
4. Move yarn slowly in an arc from one side to the other, about 6" above child's face. Pass if eyes follow 90° to midline. (Past midline; 180°)
5. Pass if child grasps rattle when it is touched to the backs or tips of fingers.
6. Pass if child continues to look where yarn disappeared or tries to see where it went. Yarn should be dropped quickly from sight from tester's hand without arm movement.
7. Pass if child picks up raisin with any part of thumb and a finger.
8. Pass if child picks up raisin with the ends of thumb and index finger using an over hand approach.

9. Pass any enclosed form. Fail continuous round motions.
10. Which line is longer? (Not bigger.) Turn paper upside down and repeat. (3/3 or 5/6)
11. Pass any crossing lines.
12. Have child copy first. If failed, demonstrate

When giving items 9, 11 and 12, do not name the forms. Do not demonstrate 9 and 11.

13. When scoring, each pair (2 arms, 2 legs, etc.) counts as one part.
14. Point to picture and have child name it. (No credit is given for sounds only.)

15. Tell child to: Give block to Mommie; put block on table; put block on floor. Pass 2 of 3. (Do not help child by pointing, moving head or eyes.)
16. Ask child: What do you do when you are cold? ..hungry? ..tired? Pass 2 of 3.
17. Tell child to: Put block on table; under table; in front of chair, behind chair. Pass 3 of 4. (Do not help child by pointing, moving head or eyes.)
18. Ask child: If fire is hot, ice is ?; Mother is a woman, Dad is a ?; a horse is big, a mouse is ?. Pass 2 of 3.
19. Ask child: What is a ball? ..lake? ..desk? ..house? ..banana? ..curtain? ..ceiling? ..hedge? ..pavement? Pass if defined in terms of use, shape, what it is made of or general category (such as banana is fruit, not just yellow). Pass 6 of 9.
20. Ask child: What is a spoon made of? ..a shoe made of? ..a door made of? (No other objects may be substituted.) Pass 3 of 3.
21. When placed on stomach, child lifts chest off table with support of forearms and/or hands.
22. When child is on back, grasp his hands and pull him to sitting. Pass if head does not hang back.
23. Child may use wall or rail only, not person. May not crawl.
24. Child must throw ball overhand 3 feet to within arm's reach of tester.
25. Child must perform standing broad jump over width of test sheet. (8-1/2 inches)
26. Tell child to walk forward, heel within 1 inch of toe. Tester may demonstrate. Child must walk 4 consecutive steps, 2 out of 3 trials.
27. Bounce ball to child who should stand 3 feet away from tester. Child must catch ball with hands, not arms, 2 out of 3 trials.
28. Tell child to walk backward, toe within 1 inch of heel. Tester may demonstrate. Child must walk 4 consecutive steps, 2 out of 3 trials.

DATE AND BEHAVIORAL OBSERVATIONS (how child feels at time of test, relation to tester, attention span, verbal behavior, self-confidence, etc,):

The DDST is a screening tool to be used to determine whether a child is not developing appropriately. It should be followed by more prescriptive instruments if the results are suspect. (*Source:* W. K. Frankenburg and J. Dodds. *Denver Developmental Screening Test.* Denver, CO: University of Colorado Medical Center, n.d.)

Figure 6–9

CHECKLIST FOR OBSERVING AND RECORDING CHILDREN'S BEHAVIOR (18–36 MONTHS)*

Child's Name ______________________ Teacher ______________________

Date of Birth ______________________ Report Date ______________________

	HAS MASTERED	*BEGINNING TO MASTER*
I. *PHYSICAL DEVELOPMENT*		
Gross-Motor Skills		
A. Has age-appropriate balance and coordination		
B. Walks alone		
C. Climbs steps with assistance (adult or stair railing)		
D. Imitates adult body movements with reasonable similarity		
E. Pushes and pulls toys (e.g., wagons and toy cars)		
F. Climbs over small obstacles		
G. Runs awkwardly		
H. Pushes self along on wheeled toy		
I. Kicks a large ball forward for a short distance		
J. Throws a small ball forward for a short distance		
Fine-Motor Skills		
K. Holds spoon, crayon, and large paintbrush		
L. Manipulates clay and fingerpaint		
M. Puts together puzzles of three to five pieces		

COMMENTS ____

____

HOME STRATEGIES ____

____

Figure 6–9 CHECKLIST FOR OBSERVING BEHAVIOR (18–36 MONTHS) (continued)

Child's Name ____________________

Date ____________________

	HAS MASTERED	BEGINNING TO MASTER
II. *COGNITIVE DEVELOPMENT*		
A. Responds to or gives first name upon request		
B. Points to or names one or more colors		
C. Points to or names two or more body parts		
D. Follows one-command directions (e.g., "Pick up the ball")		
E. Shows understanding of the purpose of objects (e.g., feeds doll with bottle or makes automobile noises while pushing toy car)		
F. Experiments with toys and other objects (e.g., attempts to insert pieces into puzzle)		
G. Has age-appropriate attention span		
H. Recalls some events or activities, such as when asked "What did you eat?"		
I. Explores new play spaces and materials		
J. Enjoys a variety of textures (e.g., sand, water, Playdough, paste)		

COMMENTS ____________________

____

HOME STRATEGIES ____________________

____

Figure 6–9 CHECKLIST FOR OBSERVING BEHAVIOR (18–36 MONTHS) (continued)

Child's Name ____________________

Date ____________________

	HAS MASTERED	BEGINNING TO MASTER
III. *LANGUAGE DEVELOPMENT*		
A. Responds when name is called		
B. Says simple words or short sentences		
C. Names familiar objects when they are pointed to		
D. Follows one-command directions (e.g., "Bring me the book")		
E. Verbalizes to adults and children		
F. Vocalizations are usually comprehensible		
G. Listens attentively to short stories		
H. Points to pictures and vocalizes		
I. Recognizes familiar sounds (e.g., responds to the ringing of a toy phone)		
J. Participates in simple finger games		
K. Attempts to say the names of others		

COMMENTS ____________________

____

HOME STRATEGIES ____________________

____

Figure 6–9 CHECKLIST FOR OBSERVING BEHAVIOR (18–36 MONTHS) (continued)

Child's Name ______________________

Date ______________________

	HAS MASTERED	*BEGINNING TO MASTER*
IV. *SOCIAL SKILLS*		
A. Can play alone at times		
B. Plays along with other children		
C. Shows ownership of toys and materials		
D. Seeks adult attention		
E. Sometimes shares adult attention		
F. Sometimes waits a short time for a turn		
G. Imitates adult behavior		
H. Occasionally follows simple classroom rules (e.g., "Please sit in your seat")		

COMMENTS ____

____

HOME STRATEGIES ____

____

Figure 6–9 CHECKLIST FOR OBSERVING BEHAVIOR (18–36 MONTHS) (continued)

Child's Name ______________________

Date ______________________

	HAS MASTERED	*BEGINNING TO MASTER*
V. *EMOTIONAL DEVELOPMENT*		
A. Sometimes cries when separating from parent(s)		
B. Is calmed or comforted by a familiar adult		
C. Seeks adults when fearful or uncertain		
D. Is normally apprehensive around strangers		
E. Expresses a broad range of emotions		
F. Expresses affection for adults		
G. Attaches to another adult (not a parent) who is a frequent caregiver		
H. Shows interest in other children		
I. Expresses hostility or anger toward others		
J. Expresses needs, likes, and dislikes		
K. Recognizes self in photograph or mirror		
L. Shows pride or pleasure when praised		

COMMENTS ______________________

____

HOME STRATEGIES ______________________

____

Figure 6–9 CHECKLIST FOR OBSERVING BEHAVIOR (18–36 MONTHS) (continued)

Child's Name ____________________

Date ____________________

	HAS MASTERED	BEGINNING TO MASTER
VI. *SELF-HELP SKILLS*		
A. Feeds self using fingers or utensils		
B. Drinks from a cup		
C. Sometimes indicates toileting needs (may be verbal or nonverbal)		
D. Tries to wash own hands		
E. Wipes mouth with napkin at mealtime		
F. Attempts to put on coat or sweater		

COMMENTS ____________________

____

HOME STRATEGIES ____________________

____

SCHOOL STRATEGIES ____________________

____

Figure 6–10

CHECKLIST FOR OBSERVING AND RECORDING CHILDREN'S BEHAVIOR (3–5 YEARS)*

Child's Name ______________________ Teacher ______________________

Date of Birth ______________________ Report Date ______________________

	HAS MASTERED	*BEGINNING TO MASTER*
I. *PHYSICAL DEVELOPMENT*		
Gross-Motor Skills		
A. Has age-appropriate balance and coordination		
B. Walks, runs, and climbs stairs with ease		
C. Moves body to music		
D. Does simple somersault		
E. Stacks and builds with blocks		
F. Imitates hopping and jumping on request		
Fine-Motor Skills		
G. Uses scissors, crayons, and paintbrushes		
H. Puts together five-to twelve-piece puzzles		
I. Uses pegboards and stacking toys easily		
J. Pours liquid from a small pitcher with little spillage		
K. Copies simple shapes		

COMMENTS ____

____

HOME STRATEGIES ____

____

*Reprinted by permission of Philadelphia Parent-Child Center.

Figure 6–10 CHECKLIST FOR OBSERVING BEHAVIOR (3–5 YEARS) (continued)

Child's Name ______________________

Date ______________________

	HAS MASTERED	BEGINNING TO MASTER
II. *COGNITIVE DEVELOPMENT*		
A. Gives own first and last names upon request		
B. Names basic shapes (square, circle, triangle)		
C. Names primary colors (red, blue, yellow)		
D. Identifies similarities and differences in objects		
E. Puts objects into sets (e.g., things with wheels)		
F. Matches identical objects or pictures		
G. Matches items that belong together (e.g., knife/fork)		
H. Counts aloud from one to ten		
I. Solves simple word problems (e.g., "What will happen if you wear your bathing suit in the snow?")		
J. Sees simple patterns in objects (e.g., leaves that are the same shape)		
K. Repeats simple patterns, such as a pattern of red, blue, and green beads		
L. Relates events in sequence		
M. Has age-appropriate attention span		
N. Sets table with one cup, napkin, plate, spoon per place		

COMMENTS ______________________

____

HOME STRATEGIES ______________________

____

Figure 6–10 CHECKLIST FOR OBSERVING BEHAVIOR (3–5 YEARS) (continued)

Child's Name ______________________

Date ______________________

	HAS MASTERED	*BEGINNING TO MASTER*
III. *LANGUAGE DEVELOPMENT*		
A. Has age-appropriate vocabulary		
B. Uses comparative terms (e.g., big/little, tall/short)		
C. Participates in conversation as both speaker and listener		
D. Follows a short sequence of verbal directions		
E. Listens attentively and recounts events from stories		
F. Names body parts		
G. Responds to questions with appropriate answers		
H. Describes persons or events shown in photographs		
I. Looks at books		
J. Recognizes and names some letters		
K. Has age-appropriate articulation		
L. Constructs and uses simple sentences		

COMMENTS ____

____

HOME STRATEGIES ____

____

Figure 6–10 CHECKLIST FOR OBSERVING BEHAVIOR (3–5 YEARS) (continued)

Child's Name ______________________

Date ______________________

	HAS MASTERED	*BEGINNING TO MASTER*
IV. *SOCIAL SKILLS*		
A. Can play alone at times		
B. Enjoys play with one or more other children		
C. Can wait briefly for own turn		
D. Occasionally shares toys or materials with others		
E. Enjoys conversation with adults and children		
F. Usually follows established rules		
G. Respects the property of other children		
H. Can lead a group		
I. Can follow another child who is group leader		
J. Enjoys playing a variety of roles in fantasy play (e.g., mother, baby, fireman, superhero, etc.)		
K. Enjoys winning games		
L. Applauds others who win		
M. Enjoys helping adults		

COMMENTS ______________________

____

HOME STRATEGIES ______________________

____

Figure 6–10 CHECKLIST FOR OBSERVING BEHAVIOR (3–5 YEARS) (continued)

Child's Name ____________________

Date ____________________

	HAS MASTERED	BEGINNING TO MASTER
V. *EMOTIONAL DEVELOPMENT*		
A. Separates easily from parent(s)		
B. Expresses a broad range of emotions		
C. Tries to describe feelings verbally		
D. Shows attachment to other children and adults		
E. Expresses affection for others		
F. Expresses hostility or anger toward others		
G. Shares adult attention with other children		
H. Clearly expresses needs, likes, and dislikes		
I. Shows ownership of toys and materials		
J. Shows pride in possessions and accomplishments		

COMMENTS ____________________

____

HOME STRATEGIES ____________________

____

Figure 6–10 CHECKLIST FOR OBSERVING BEHAVIOR (3–5 YEARS) (continued)

Child's Name ______________________

Date ______________________

	HAS MASTERED	*BEGINNING TO MASTER*
VI. ***SELF-HELP SKILLS***		
A. Dresses self in coat, socks, shoes		
B. Washes and dries own hands		
C. Brushes teeth		
D. Uses fork and spoon		
E. Serves self at mealtimes		
F. Sets and clears own place at table		
G. Wipes mouth with napkin after meals		
H. Toilets self unassisted		
I. Fastens clothing after toileting		
J. Asks for adult assistance as needed		

COMMENTS ______________________

____

HOME STRATEGIES ______________________

____

SCHOOL STRATEGIES ______________________

____

Figure 6–11

SAMPLE ANECDOTAL RECORDS

SUBJECT: JAMES   DATE: 10/15/88   TIME 9:50–9:45 A.M.

James is three years old. He has been in our classroom for four months. This morning children had free-choice time between 9:30 and 10:00 A.M. All of the children selected areas in which they wanted to play except James; he stood quietly in the corner of the classroom sucking his thumb. When another child approached and tried to engage him in play, saying, "Want to build with the blocks?" James nodded "no" and moved farther into the corner. James followed other children's movements with his eyes. When he heard a child singing a familiar song, he mouthed the words. However, for the remainder of free-choice time James stayed in the corner.

Summary: Since the time of his enrollment in the program, James has resisted play and involvement with other children. Despite the efforts of the teachers to get him to participate, James pulls away from other children and avoids talking to them. He does speak occasionally to the teachers, especially to ask for food or a drink. He also indicates by body movements that he wants to hold a teacher's hand or sit on his or her lap. James needs assistance to gradually begin relating to other children, at first on a one-to-one basis and later in a group.

SUBJECT: SUSAN L.   DATE: 11/21/88   TIME: 10:10–10:50 A.M.

Susan is a five year old in our classroom. She will be ready for kindergarten in the fall. Susan is playing in the housekeeping area. She has two playmates, Aaron and Jack. The two boys call her "mother," and Susan pretends to fix and serve a meal at the play stove. All goes well in their dramatic play until Jack says that he would like to be the "mommy." Susan begins shouting at him and crying. She says, "I'm the mommy! I'm the mommy!" When Jack says that he wants to have a turn, Susan begins hitting him and rushes to the teacher saying, "Jack won't let me be mommy anymore."

Summary: Susan has shown here and on previous occasions her reluctance to assume less dominant roles during play. She becomes observably distressed when asked to step down from a leadership role and clearly needs assistance to assume other roles during play.

Figure 6–12

ACCIDENT REPORT/ILLNESS FORM

Date ________

Name of Injured Person ______________________________ Child ______
Staff ______
Visitor ______

Address ______________________________

Birth Date ________________

Male ______ Female ______

Telephone ____________

GIVE DETAILS CONCERNING THE ACCIDENT

Date of Accident ________________ Time of Accident ________________

Location Where Occurred ______________________________

Describe the Accident ______________________________

____

____

____

Name of Person(s) Witnessing the Accident ______________________________

____

____

First-Aid Action ______________________________

____

Referral to Hospital ______________________________

____

Referral to Physician ______________________________

Figure 6–12 ACCIDENT REPORT/ILLNESS FORM (continued)

How Transported ______________________________

Name of Person Transporting ______________________________

Other Pertinent Information Concerning Injured Person and Accident

____

____

____

____

____

Figure 6–13

SUGGESTIONS FOR PARENT CONFERENCES

1. Find a mutual time when both you and parents will be unhurried
2. Provide an informal setting for your meeting
3. Meet in a private place whenever possible
4. Prepare beforehand by collecting anecdotal records, papers, and artwork
5. Establish a time limit, but adjust the conference to meet the parents' needs
6. Introduce yourself if you don't know one another
7. Do not let your desk function as a barricade between you and parents
8. Begin and end the conference with a positive comment about the child
9. Develop an attitude of mutual cooperation and respect
10. Express appreciation for the opportunity of working with the parents
11. Assure parents of the confidentiality of information discussed
12. Use the conference to develop a partnership between you and the parents
13. Find out how the parents think and feel about their child
14. Hear criticism fully and select suggestions
15. Avoid your opinions about the child's behavior; state only the facts
16. Be sincere—show genuine concern
17. Listen more; talk less
18. Be supportive and encouraging
19. Do not be judgmental
20. Check your body language; be alert to parents' body language
21. In concluding the meeting, seek parental input for solutions to help the child
22. Keep a written record of the meeting; provide one copy of the record to the parent and keep one on file

Figure 6–14

PARENT CONFERENCE REPORT

Date ____________

Mr. and Mrs. John Smith
35 Good Street
City, Pennsylvania 19030

RE: JAMES

Dear Mr. and Mrs. Smith:

As promised, I am summarizing the main points of our conference on Thursday when we discussed James's achievements and what he needs to do to improve his language skills and feeling of competence.

We agreed that at home you will:

1. Show an interest in what James has to say;
2. Answer, giving clear, descriptive, full statements in response;
3. Encourage him to listen and to explore by feeling, smelling, seeing, and tasting whenever possible;
4. Read to him and tell him stories; and
5. Provide a quiet place for him to enjoy books on his own.

I will record his developments in the same areas at the center so we may share evidence of his growth.

Your help in listening to James, talking with him, reading to him, and allowing him opportunities for self-exploration will be of great assistance to his learning.

Please call me if you have any questions. If I do not hear from you, I will contact you, as we agreed, in three weeks and report how James is progressing at the center.

Thank you for your assistance.

Sincerely,

____
(Teacher)

Figure 6–15

REPORT ON PARENT CONFERENCE

Child's Name ______________________________ Date ____________

Parent(s) Name ______________________________

Problems Identified ______________________________

____

____

____

Solutions Planned for Problems ______________________________

____

____

____

____

Activities for Parents ______________________________

____

____

____

____

Objectives to Be Met ______________________________

____

____

____

____

Comments ______________________________

____

____

____

Further Reading

AMERICAN ACADEMY OF PEDIATRICS. *Standards of Child Health Care.* Evanston, IL: American Academy of Pediatrics, 1972.

BERGER, E.H. *Parents as Partners in Education,* p. 93. St. Louis, MO: C.V. Mosby, 1981.

DAVIS, A. *Let's Have Healthy Children,* rev. ed. New York: Signet, 1981.

DINKMEYER, D., and G. D. MCKAY. *Parents' Handbook,* Circle Pines, MN: American Guidance Service, 1983.

FRANKENBURG, W.K. *Denver Prescreening Developmental Questionnaire.* Denver, University of Colorado Medical Center, 1975.

GREEN, M.I. *A Sigh of Relief: First Aid Handbook For Childhood Emergencies,* rev. ed. New York: Bantam Press, 1984.

MILLER, B.L., and A.L. WILMSHURST. *Parents and Volunteers in the Classroom: A Handbook for Teachers.* San Francisco: R.E. Associates, 1975.

School Volunteer Programs: Everything You Need to Know to Start or Improve Your Program. Alexandria, VA: National School Volunteer Program, 1981.

SEEFELDT, C. *"Parent Involvement: Support or Stress?" Childhood Education,* November/December 1985, pp. 98–102.

section 7

PUBLIC RELATIONS FOR EARLY CHILDHOOD EDUCATION

The forms and examples in this section feature an assortment of public-relations tools and range from ideas and techniques for recruitment to suggestions for networking with the community.

THE BUSINESS OF EARLY CHILDHOOD EDUCATION

The early childhood program of the 1980s and 1990s is not merely a school or a place of attentive caregiving, it is also a business. Even when a program has nonprofit status, it is still a viable and active part of the business community. As a business, the early childhood program extends itself into and influences the community as a whole. It opens itself to scrutiny and feedback, if the center wishes to participate fully in the community. This means that the center's director urges members of the community to visit the center, and the media is utilized fully to advise the community of ongoing activities and events. Early childhood programs have some obligation to represent the profession in its most positive light, especially at a time when there are many misconceptions about problems within preschool and day care programs.

RECRUITMENT AND PROMOTION

When recruitment of clients (children and parents) is the aim of the program, an administrator should carefully consider all possible client sources (see Figure 7–1) and carefully select the advertising medium and language. These choices are very much influenced by the type of information to be disseminated. For example, newspaper advertisements are an excellent mechanism for recruitment. Newspaper space, however, is costly, and words must be chosen carefully in order to convey key points about a program. Figure 7–2 illustrates a newspaper ad.

For generating inquiries about the program, strategically placed posters can also be very effective. A photograph of teachers or caregivers involved with children can serve to further heighten interest in a center. Figure 7–3 presents a sample recruitment poster.

Every program and family day care home should have a brochure. An outline of the agency or provider's services, typed or neatly printed on a piece of paper and made more interesting with a photograph or drawing, can do wonders for both recruitment and image within the community. This need not be an expensive venture, as the brochures can be duplicated on a copy machine. A sample recruitment and informational brochure is shown in Figure 7–4.

In most small and many large communities, the radio, television, and newspapers can be great friends and allies of the early childhood program. The media actively seek out human-interest stories, and the public is generally interested in children. Special events, such as holiday parties and trips, can often fill a closing spot on the evening news. It is advisable for program administrators to cultivate relationships with members of the media and to suggest to them (rather than wait for an expression of interest in) events at the center.

When printed material is utilized to advertise or publicize a program, as in the sample shown in Figure 7–5, it is essential that considerable thought be given to language and content used. Obviously, an administrator should emphasize valuable points: the unique or special services that a program provides. Furthermore, aspects of licensure or registration of a program, training and skill of staff, and parameters of curriculum should also be briefly outlined. Language used should be clear and to the point, and the individual preparing public-relations materials should make sure that all posters, brochures, and newspaper advertisements provide information consistent with program policy. It is extraordinarily disconcerting for a parent to discover that advertising literature has been misleading or promotes a service no longer available.

A center newsletter like that illustrated in Figure 7–6 can be an extremely positive avenue for public relations. The newsletters should be attractive in appearance, with short and informative articles. It offers opportunities for expanded coverage of policies, activities, events, and concerns of all of the persons involved in the program. Furthermore, "friends of the center," such as policy board members, past or graduate parents, and business and community leaders can be kept updated via a regularly disseminated newsletter. Newsletters can also be an effective means for parental involvement. Not only can parents be urged to contribute articles and ideas, but in many cases they should be urged to edit the newsletter. Children as well should be asked to contribute.

VOLUNTEERS

A good public-relations campaign can also draw volunteers. Knowing that a program serves young children, that it is in good standing in the community, and that it receives attention from the media provides incentive for those who are looking for a place to invest spare time. Volunteers enjoy being able to say, "Yes, that is my program."

Volunteers may be recruited from a broad spectrum of community members using some of the recruitment ideas in Figure 7–7. While senior citizens are some of the most likely candidates due to their flexibility of working hours, there are other potential volunteer populations that should not be overlooked. College students with human-service majors are prime candidates for volunteer services. Consider students in early childhood education, child development, home economics, and child welfare as potential volunteers. Local high-school students with interests in these areas should also be considered. Classroom volunteers may also be found among the members of Scout troops and community-service organizations.

It should be recognized that some volunteers are needed or wanted in places other than the classroom. Volunteers can be individuals utilized for fundraising, clerical, maintenance, and other important program needs. While some individuals wishing to volunteer may not have many hours to spare, their potential contribution should not be overlooked. Individuals with unique skills or expertise (plumbers, electricians, physicians, and lawyers) provide invaluable, if only occasional services.

Figures 7–8 through 7–10 present several different kinds of aids for use with volunteers, including a volunteer application form, a volunteer orientation and training agenda, and a volunteer sign-in sheet.

PLANNING FOR PUBLIC RELATIONS

In conclusion, a campaign of public relations should be considered a critical aspect of program development. We urge program administrators and family day care providers to develop a plan for this component of their programs, just as they plan for parental involvement and for curriculum. Furthermore, the success of public-relations efforts should be regularly evaluated and modifications made as need indicates.

At the advent of the twenty-first century, as early childhood programs achieve importance in the lives of children and their parents, it becomes increasingly necessary for these programs to assume their place in the business and professional community. In doing so, child-care providers are most clearly able to maintain the quality of programs, increase public awareness of the services provided, and serve as advocates for the needs of the American family.

Figure 7–1

CLIENT RECRUITMENT IDEAS

Possible sources for recruitment of day care clients are

1. Newspaper advertisements
2. Peel-off referrals placed in infant clothing stores, supermarkets, child dentistry offices, children's shoe stores
3. Public schools
4. Private schools
5. Unemployment service offices
6. Churches, synagogues, mosques (in newsletters, on bulletin boards)
7. Teacher-affiliated groups
8. Professional organizations
9. Civic clubs
10. Ethnic societies
11. Laundromats
12. Community centers
13. Signs in car windows
14. Information and referral services
15. Health food stores
16. Word-of-mouth

Figure 7–2

SAMPLE NEWSPAPER ADVERTISEMENT

GRANT DAY CARE CENTER

(215) 700–6000

37 EAST MAIN STREET

Welcome to an open house of parents of day care and preschool-aged children.

Thursday and Friday, March 10 and 11
8:30 A.M. to 11:00 A.M.

Tour the center, meet with our certified training staff and administrators, and learn about our program.

REFRESHMENTS SERVED

Figure 7–3

SAMPLE RECRUITMENT POSTER

REGISTER NOW
FOR EARLY ENROLLMENT
SPRING 1989

GRANT DAY CARE CENTER & PRESCHOOL

- HOURS 7:00 A.M.–6:00 P.M.
- HOT MEALS INCLUDED
- SMALL CLASSES
- FULLY EQUIPPED PLAYGROUND
- DEGREED STAFF
- STATE LICENSED & APPROVED
- MINIMUM WEEKLY FEE

(215) 700-6000
37 EAST MAIN STREET
CITY, PENNSYLVANIA

Figure 7–4

SAMPLE RECRUITMENT
AND INFORMATIONAL BROCHURE

[**Cover Page**]

[Name of Center]
[Address of Center]
[Telephone Number of Center]

[Name of Director]

[**Page One**]

Registration

Parents and children are encouraged to visit the center during any morning session to visit the facility and observe the program. All application forms with appropriate explanation will be made available at this time. Parents' questions about entrance requirements will be answered.

It is important that parents schedule their visit at least two weeks prior to the child's entrance into a full day's routine. This method allows a period of adjustment for the child, other children, and staff.

Eligibility

[Center Name] is a year-round, full day care service for preschool children aged three to five. A child must have received all of the required dosages of immunizations before he or she can be admitted to the classroom. Children must also be toilet trained.

Schedule

The center operates from 7 A.M. to 6 P.M. Monday through Friday, twelve months a year. The educational program is planned to begin at 8:30 A.M. Parents are encouraged to have their children present by this time. Listen to radio station TALK 3 for information concerning emergency closings due to inclement weather, no heat, and unanticipated emergencies. The center is closed for the following holidays: New Year's Day, Martin Luther King's Birthday, Memorial Day, Independence Day, Labor Day, Thanksgiving Day, and Christmas Day.

Figure 7–4 SAMPLE RECRUITMENT AND INFORMATIONAL BROCHURE (continued)

Fees

Our center operates strictly on tuition payments paid by the families of children enrolled in our program. Families pay on a sliding-fee scale.

Payments are due and payable every Monday. Absences are nondeductable.

Registration fee required: $________

Program

The program is based on goals, objectives, and activities aimed at providing a flexible, enriching environment that will facilitate the physical, cognitive, and social-emotional growth of children aged three to five. The program is supervised at all times by an experienced, certified, and credentialed staff.

There is an equal balance of active and quiet periods, fine-motor and gross-motor activities, indoor and outdoor times, individual and group activities, and teacher-directed activities and child-initiated activities.

The food-service program provides well-balanced, nutritional meals that meet local, state, and federal guidelines established by the Department of Agriculture.

Afternoon rest periods are planned and provided for. Transportation to and from school is the responsibility of the parent(s).

The center director has an open-door policy and is available to discuss parents' concerns. Please feel free to contact the director to arrange a mutual meeting time.

Figure 7–5

SAMPLE PUBLICITY RELEASE* FORMAT

GRANT day
care
association

NEWS RELEASE

SEARCHING FOR QUALITY CHILD CARE?
HERE IT IS!

LOCATION:	Convenient to public transportation, center city, and all expressways–situated in the heart of mainstream, Village Hill Road & Greenway Avenue.
FACILITIES:	Childproof activity rooms, indoor pool, secure indoor/outdoor play area, fully equipped classrooms and playground, and arts and crafts area you must see.
PROGRAM:	Learning and play activities that promote cognitive, social and emotional, and physical development for infant/toddlers and preschoolers–full time.
STAFF:	Certified and credentialed staff who are committed to creating and maintaining a structured, caring setting where children can learn and grow at their own pace.
VALUE:	Some of the lowest rates in the area.

Call us. We'll be happy to show you around.
234-6000 234-6300

---

*This release is the kind used when a center or agency wants to receive publicity via an article in a newspaper, magazine, or through a radio or TV announcement. The publicity release provides basic information that can be used to round out a story about the program. The publicity-release package should include:

1. "Cover" release—presenting the fundamental facts of your story
2. "Backgrounder" release—providing additional information to put the story in perspective (history of organization or key points)
3. "Remarks"—giving the center a forum for commenting on the significance of its news
4. Text of the statement
5. Release biography of the center
6. Supporting literature
7. Pertinent photographs

Figure 7–6

SAMPLE NEWSLETTER

VOICE *from the Center*

AFRO-AMERICAN FEDERATION DAY CARE CENTER NOV.–DEC. VOL II NO. 4

REPORT FROM THE DIRECTOR

We have a serious problem. On November 1st, we were expecting $30,000 from the state, but it still has not arrived. As a consequence, we were only able to pay staff half of what we owed them. Worse yet is the strong probability that the money to pay them and our many other bills may not arrive until January. Imagine working more than a month without pay!

Even though we are working under this serious handicap, the Center has made tremendous progress during the last four months. We now have our own Tax Number which should end our problems with the Internal Revenue Service. Our mail is now delivered directly to the Day Care Center, and the A.A.F. Board of Directors has agreed to incorporate the Day Care Center as a separate legal body. Also, we now have the control of our checkbook, when there is money in it. And, the Center has a new Director, a new Head Teacher, a new Social Worker, a new Secretary, and a new Bookkeeper. We are strengthening our health component with the help of Covenant Health Services, Inc.

Our Teaching Staff members are now attending a series of training workshops designed to help them work more effectively with your children. The Parents' Policy Board has crystallized its memberships, and communications, I hope, have improved with the printing of this newsletter. Last but not least, we now have a full tank of heating oil, a thousand gallons that might last eight weeks.

VOTER REGISTRATION

Voter Registration is now going on. If you wish to change your party registration, this is the time to do it!

THANKSGIVING FEAST

Oh, did Miss Mary outdo herself in the kitchen for the Second Annual Thanksgiving Feast! Thanks to the parents who provided the luscious desserts that were a fitting end to Mary's culinary artistry. The thanks of the staff are extended to those parents who helped make it all possible.

PARENTS' AIDE CENTER

The Parent Policy Board at their December 3rd meeting, with 19 people in attendance, decided to petition the Board of Education and the Regional State Welfare Office for the funds that are overdue to our center. A telegram was also sent to Mr. Terry Dellmuth, Governor Shapp's Special Assistant for Human Services. Parents have also agreed to ask the A.A.F. Board to take a loan to pay staff. The parents group will try to raise funds to cover the interest.

OVERHEARD IN THE CLASSROOM

As the three year olds made their way to the library on one of their bi-monthly trips, the children passed a firetruck. All of them exclaimed in delight and Miss Kathy commented, "Do you see the fireman?" "Oh, he's just a cop with big boots," said little Arshell Stokes with disinterest.

ACTIVITY OF THE MONTH

Since the Holiday Season brings thoughts of turkey dinners with it, why not have the children make their own turkeys? One way to do this is to fashion the turkey from clay. First take *moist* clay (or Playdough) and have the children "roll a ball" (this will be the body). Second, take another piece of moist clay and have the children "make a pancake" (this will be the tail). Third, put the ball (body) and the pancake (tail) together. Fourth, have the children "roll a big snake and a little snake" (the big one is for the head and neck and the little one is for the gobbler). Fifth, put the big snake (head and neck) on the body and then attach the gobbler to the head (this gives the turkey effect). Six, let dry. Seven, paint. By having the children manipulate the clay, you will help them increase the fine-motor coordination in their fingers.

by Mary Ann

NEW SECRETARY

Staff and parents extend a warm welcome to the newest member of the Day Care Center staff, Mrs. Elizabeth Alston, who is filling the position of secretary. Mrs. Alston is the mother of two girls and is married to a sales representative of Moore Business Forms, Inc.

HELP

Volunteers are needed to accompany our children to the Enchanted Village on December 12th and to Wanamakers on December 17th. Those interested please contact the Center.

CHRISTMAS PARTY

A Christmas Party for our children is planned for December 21st at 12:30. Parents are to provide refreshments, and a visit from Santa is expected.

A.A.F. BOARD MEETING

Parents and Staff are welcome at the December 10th, 8 p.m., A.A.F. Board Meeting to be held at our center.

NEW ARRIVAL

Congratulations are due to Mr. and Mrs. Chestnut on the birth of Abdul Malik, born November 7th. The new arrival weighed in at a healthy 6 pounds and 6 ounces.

EDITORIAL COMMENT

Speaking to you as a parent, I would like to stress the importance of attendance at the monthly parents' meetings. Only four parents were present at the November 5th gathering. Of course, none of us will be able to attend every meeting. We all have responsibilities at home, but it must be stressed that these are critical times in the life of our Center. In order to survive, we must all be as involved as possible. We have an obligation to fa-

Figure 7–6 SAMPLE NEWSLETTER (continued)

miliarize ourselves with the way our Center works and take an active part in its government. The best way to do this is to attend meetings scheduled at the Center whenever possible.

by Kathy

REMINDER

Parents, please be sure that the person picking up or delivering your child is at least 12 years old. We don't want any accidents to happen during travel time.

N.B. Any parent with a grievance should contact a member of the Grievance Committee.

Carolyn	VI9–4046
Mary	VI9–8978
Shirley	GE8–1144

Figure 7–7

VOLUNTEER RECRUITMENT IDEAS
ADOPT-A-CLASS
GRANT DAY CARE CENTER

Dear Parents:
We need volunteers to help our program continue to grow. Please adopt a class and participate in the activities of your choice. Please circle your preferences from the list below.

	HOME	*CLASSROOM*	*RESOURCE-MATERIALS CENTER*
1. Be a room-parent facilitator			
2. Read to children			
3. Tell stories to children			
4. Share your recipes			
5. Work as a transportation monitor			
6. Make books with children			
7. Play games with children			
8. Assist in the resource center			
9. Help select books for children			
10. Listen to children			
11. Assist in learning centers			
12. Prepare bulletin boards			
13. Plan workshops for parents			
14. Collect recyclables			
15. Make games for children			
16. Write newsletters			
17. Coordinate volunteers			
18. Reproduce materials on copier			
19. Serve on telephone committee			
20. Serve on baby-sitting committee			

Areas of interest not listed? ____________________

Comments ____________________

Figure 7–7 VOLUNTEER RECRUITMENT IDEAS (continued)

TIME AVAILABLE	*A.M.*	*P.M.*
Monday		
Tuesday		
Wednesday		
Thursday		
Friday		
Saturday		

Name ______________________________ Telephone ____________

Date ______________

Figure 7–8

VOLUNTEER APPLICATION FORM

Date ____________

Name ________________ ________________ Telephone ____________
last first

Address ____
street

____
city state zip code

Have you had a chest X-ray or tine test within the past three years? ______

Have you obtained the required request for criminal history record/ application for child-abuse history? ______

Please cite the areas in which you would like to assist in the classroom:

ENRICHMENT CENTERS

1. ____ Woodworking
2. ____ Housekeeping
3. ____ Science
4. ____ Water play
5. ____ Sand
6. ____ Modeling materials (clay, sawdust, paper-mâché)
7. ____ Paint
8. ____ Music/movement
9. ____ Manipulative materials
10. ____ Books/stories
11. ____ Pastel/collage
12. ____ Foods
13. ____ Social studies (child self-concept, communications skills)
14. ____ Collect recyclables
15. ____ Make games for children
16. ____ Write newsletters
17. ____ Coordinate volunteers
18. ____ Reproduce materials on copier
19. ____ Serve on telephone committee
20. ____ Serve on baby-sitting committee

Figure 7–8 VOLUNTEER APPLICATION FORM (continued)

TIME AVAILABLE	*A.M.*	*P.M.*
Monday		
Tuesday		
Wednesday		
Thursday		
Friday		
Saturday		

Figure 7–9

VOLUNTEER ORIENTATION AND TRAINING AGENDA

I. Registration

II. Refreshments/Informal Fellowship

III. Welcome

- **A.** Introduction of Center staff

IV. Brief Overview of Center Program

- **A.** Program objectives
- **B.** Organizational structure
- **C.** Policies and procedures (Handbooks to be distributed)

V. The Volunteer Program

- **A.** Acknowledgement/appreciation of volunteers
- **B.** Goals of volunteer program
- **C.** Benefits of volunteer program to children, parents, staff, and community

VI. Roles of Volunteers

- **A.** Requirements
  - **1.** Health assessment
  - **2.** State/local criminal-history check
  - **3.** Attendance
  - **4.** Supervision
  - **5.** Training
- **B.** Description of available volunteer jobs
  - **1.** Responsibilities
  - **2.** Work schedule

VII. Questions and Answers, Comments and Concerns

VIII. Registration of Volunteers

Figure 7–10

VOLUNTEER SIGN-IN SHEET

I. Name ______________________________ Date ____________

TIME

FROM ________ *TO* ________

Monday
Tuesday
Wednesday
Thursday
Friday

Duties ____
____
____
____

______________________ Volunteer's Signature

______________________ Director's Signature

II. Materials, Supplies, Equipment

I attest that I have contributed the following:

Description	Amount	Total

______________________ Date

______________________ Donor's Signature

______________________ Director's Signature

Figure 7–11

SUGGESTIONS FOR NETWORKING WITH THE COMMUNITY

I. Clarify and make known to the public your center's purpose by:

1. Designing advertisements for all forms of media
2. Speaking to citizen's groups
3. Informing local human-services agencies
4. Informing the public, private, and parochial school systems
5. Using public-service spots on radio and TV
6. Listing/describing your center and its program in local, regional, and state service directories
7. Posting a descriptive sign at your center highlighting its purpose

II. Identify all community agencies (health, social, welfare, legal, psychological), businesses, churches, synagogues, mosques, professional individuals and groups, colleges, sororities, fraternities, VFW's, American Legions, stores (small and large), etc., that might be of assistance to your program.

1. Make a schematic diagram of all the aforementioned
2. Learn about their purposes, goals, and policies
3. Arrange an appointment to interview a key staff person
   - **a.** Indicate how their services meet your needs
   - **b.** Invite key agency representatives to your center
   - **c.** Establish an open, trusting, and mutually beneficial relationship
   - **d.** Discuss realistic time frames in which services can be rendered
   - **e.** Develop feedback systems
   - **f.** Plan strategies to ensure that cooperation and collaboration can easily take place for all concerned
   - **g.** Maintain a file on all agencies/individuals who provide services, goods, and funds to your center

III. Provide written expressions of gratitude to everyone who helps your center in any fashion.

Further Reading

BROCK, H.C. *Parent Volunteer Programs in Early Childhood Education: A Practical Guide*. Hamden, CT: Shoestring Press, 1976.

DASILVA, B., and R.D. LUCAS. *Practical School Volunteer and Teacher-Aide Programs*. West Nyack, NY: Parker Publishing, 1974.

DINKMEYER, D. and G.D. MCKAY. *Parent's Handbook*. Circle Pines, MN: American Guidance Service, 1983.

DURANT, L., and K.P. WATKINS. *Preschool Director's Staff Development Handbook*. West Nyack, NY: The Center for Applied Research In Education, 1987.

FREUND, J.W. *Coordinator's Guide: Volunteers and Volunteer Services in School*. Winnetka, IL: Winnetka Public Schools.

MILLER, B.L., and A.L. WILMSHURST. *Parents and Volunteers in the Classroom: A Handbook for Teachers*. San Francisco: R & E Research Associates, 1975.

School Volunteer Programs: Everything You Need to Know to Start or Improve Your Program. Alexandria, VA: National School Volunteer Program, 1981.

section 8

RESOURCES FOR EARLY CHILDHOOD EDUCATION

This last section of *The Complete Book of Forms for Managing the Early Childhood Program* presents a list of some of the many resources available to early childhood educators. The value of knowing what is available to foster the development of your program cannot be overemphasized.

TYPES OF PROGRAMS

As we visit day care and preschool centers in Pennsylvania and observe others across the country, we tend to see two very different types of programs. Some administrators and staff are content to maintain the status quo. Policies and practices instituted at the time a program was started are often in effect years later. There is little staff turnover, but there is also little staff development. Staff members are usually unhappy. They tend to express serious job dissatisfaction and may talk often of goals that have little to do with educating young children. Parents have little to do with the program, except seeing it as a place to drop off and pick up their children. Parents' meetings are poorly attended. Administrators are more than overworked; they are angry. They get little support for their efforts from others involved in the program.

The second type of center we see in our travels stands in marked contrast to the first. The staff has the ordinary complaints that accompany hard work, but they are discussed with humor, not bitterness. Instead there is a sense of camaraderie and enjoyment of each day spent together and with the children. Parents are visible everywhere, helping during the day and donating items for the center and classroom. Yes, directors of these centers are overworked, too. Yet there is a fundamental difference in how they feel about their roles. They are more relaxed administrators because they count on staff and parents to help meet the many needs of the program. They also know that there is a wide world of persons, places, and things—RESOURCES—available to help meet the growing needs of their programs, staff, and families.

THE VALUE OF RESOURCES

We do not mean to oversimplify. Resources do not account entirely for the sharp contrast between the two types of programs described above. They are, however, an extremely influential factor in program quality.

What are resources? Any influential people, places, or things found outside a program that can or do lend their expertise, information, or other type of assistance to the program are resources. Of course, there are persons within each agency that have special talents or expertise, but in this section we want to alert readers to resources outside their programs.

Resources can be found everywhere. They exist in our own communities. Among the civic leaders, public schools, businesses, museums, and other facilities and persons found in every town and city are resources that can be used by early childhood centers. They also exist on a national scale in even greater numbers. This section identifies some of the organizations, state offices, publishers, and manufacturers that can be utilized by early childhood programs.

Resources can help us solve problems within a program. They provide individuals, information, and sites that help to answer the many questions that arise in the course of operating an early childhood program.

Resources let us know we are not alone. Many programs share common concerns.

Resources provide a means of sharing administrative and teaching responsibilities. Resources that are available to all staff become mechanisms for personnel to work together to meet human and other needs.

Resources can teach. They can suggest to us the ideas we have not yet thought of. They can ask us to try something novel, or to stop to learn about something new.

Finally, resources are like a breath of fresh air that keeps everyone alert, interested, and growing together. After all, how can we support, nurture, or educate young children if we are not supported, nurtured, and educated ourselves?

STATE OFFICES FOR CHILD CARE LICENSING

Office of Program Administration
64 North Union Street
Montgomery, Alabama 36130

Department of Health and Social Services
Pouch H-05
Juneau, Alaska 99811

Arizona Department of Health Services
1740 West Adams
Phoenix, Arizona 85007

Department of Social and Rehabilitative Services
744 P Street
Mail Station 17-17
Sacramento, California 95814

Department of Social Services
1575 Sherman Street
Room 420
Denver, Colorado 80203

State Department of Health
79 Elm Street
Hartford, Connecticut 06115

Department of Health and Social Services
P.O. Box 309
Wilmington, Delaware 19899

Department of Human Services
1905 E Street S.E.
5th Floor
Washington, D.C. 20003

Department of Health and Rehabilitative Services
1311 Winewood Boulevard
Tallahassee, Florida 32301

Department of Human Resources
618 Ponce de Leon Avenue
Atlanta, Georgia 30308

Division of Social Services
P.O. Box 2816
Agana, Guam 96910

Department of Social Services and Housing
P.O. Box 339
Honolulu, Hawaii 96809

Department of Health and Welfare
Statehouse
Boise, Idaho 83720

Department of Children and Family Services
1 North Old State Capital Plaza
Springfield, Illinois 62706

State Department of Public Welfare
100 North Senate Avenue
Room 701
Indianapolis, Indiana 46204

Department of Social Services
3619½ Douglass Avenue
Des Moines, Iowa 50310

Division of Health and Environment
Building 740
Forbes AFB
Topeka, Kansas 66620

Department of Human Resources
Fourth Floor East
275 East Main Street
Frankfort, Kentucky 40601

Department of Health and Human Resources
P.O. Box 3767
Baton Rouge, Louisiana 70821

Department of Human Services
Augusta, Maine 04333

Department of Health and Mental Hygiene
201 West Preston Street
Baltimore, Maryland 21201

Office for Children
120 Boylston Street
Boston, Massachusetts 02116

Michigan Department of Social Services
116 West Allegan
P.O. Box 80037
Lansing, Michigan 48926

Department of Public Welfare
Centennial Office Building
4th Floor
St. Paul, Minnesota 55155

State Board of Health
P.O. Box 1700
Jackson, Mississippi 39205

State Department of Social Services
Broadway State Office Building
303 W. McCarthy Street
Jefferson City, Missouri 65103

Montana Department of Social and Rehabilitative Services
P.O. Box 4210
Helena, Montana 59601

Department of Public Welfare
P.O. Box 95026
Lincoln, Nebraska 68509

Division of Youth Services
505 East King Street
Carson City, Nevada 89710

Office of Social Services
Hazen Drive
Concord, New Hampshire 03301

New Jersey Department of Human Services
1 South Montgomery Street
Trenton, New Jersey 08623

Health and Environment Department
725 St. Michael's Drive
P.O. Box 968
Santa Fe, New Mexico 87503

Health and Environment Department
P.O. Box 2348
Room 519
Pera Building
7th and New Mexico
Santa Fe, New Mexico 87501

New York State Department of Social Services
40 North Pearl Street
Albany, New York 12243

Office of Child Day Care Licensing
P.O. Box 10157
1915 Ridge Road
Raleigh, North Carolina 27065

Child and Family Services
Russell Building
Box 7
Highway 83 North
Bismarck, North Dakota 58505

Bureau of Licensing and Standards
30 E. Broad Street
30th Floor
Columbus, Ohio 43215

Department of Public Welfare
P.O. Box 25352
Oklahoma City, Oklahoma 73125

Department of Human Resources
198 Commercial Street S.E.
Salem, Oregon 97310

Pennsylvania Department of Public Welfare
Room 423
Health and Welfare Building
Harrisburg, Pennsylvania 17120

P.O. Box 11398
Fernandez Juncos Station
Santurce, Puerto Rico 00910

Department of Social and
Rehabilitative Services
610 Mount Pleasant Avenue
Providence, Rhode Island 02908

South Carolina Department of
Social Services
P.O. Box 1520
Columbia, South Carolina 29202

Department of Social Services
Richard F. Kneip Building
Pierre, South Dakota 57501

Tennessee Department of Human
Services
111-9 7th Avenue North
Nashville, Tennessee 37203

Texas Department of Human
Resources
P.O. Box 2960
Austin, Texas 78769

Division of Family Services
P.O. Box 2500
Salt Lake City, Utah 84100

Department of Social and
Rehabilitative Services
81 River Street
Montpelier, Vermont 05602

Department of Welfare
8007 Discovery Drive
Richmond, Virginia 23229

Department of Social Services
P.O. Box 539
Charlotte Amalie
St. Thomas, Virgin Islands 00801

The Department of Social and
Health Services
State Office Building #2
Mail Stop 440
Olympia, Washington 98504

Department of Welfare
1900 Washington Street East
Charleston, West Virginia 25305

Division of Community Services
1 West Wilson Street
Madison, Wisconsin 53702

Division of Public Assistance and
Social Services
Hathaway Building
Cheyenne, Wyoming 82002

SOURCES OF INFORMATION ON GRANTS AND FUNDING

Education Funding Research
Council
75 National Press Building N.W.
Washington, D.C. 20045

Education News Services Division
Capitol Publications, Inc.
Suite G-128
2430 Pennsylvania Avenue N.W.
Washington, D.C. 20037

The Foundation Center
1001 Connecticut Avenue N.W.
Washington, D.C. 20035

The Foundation Center
888 Seventh Avenue
New York, New York 10019

The Grantsmanship Center
1015 West Olympic Boulevard
Los Angeles, California 90015

Human Resources Network
2010 Chancellor Street
Philadelphia, Pennsylvania 19103

National Rural Center
1828 L Street N.W.
Washington, D.C. 20036

Public Management Institute
333 Hayes Street
San Francisco, California 94102

Responsive Procurement Exchange
1204 Half Street S.W.
Washington, D.C. 20024

Taft Corporation
1000 Vermont Avenue N.W.
Washington, D.C. 20005

Publications on Funding Sources/Grant Availability

American Education/Guide to
Office of Education
Administered Programs
Department of Education
Washington, D.C. 20202

Catalog of Federal Domestic
Assistance
Superintendent of Documents
U.S. Government Printing Office
Washington, D.C. 20402

Commerce Business Daily
Superintendent of Documents
U.S. Government Printing Office
Washington, D.C. 20402

Federal Register
Superintendent of Documents
U.S. Government Printing Office
Washington, D.C. 20402

ORGANIZATIONS FOR EARLY CHILDHOOD/CHILD CARE PERSONNEL

American Association of School
Administrators
1801 North Moore Street
Arlington, Virginia 22209

American Educational Research
Association
1230 17th Street N.W.
Washington, D.C. 20036

American Federation of Teachers
11 DuPont Circle N.W.
Washington, D.C. 20036

American Home Economics
Association
2010 Massachusetts Avenue N.W.
Washington, D.C. 20036

American Montessori Association
150 Fifth Avenue
New York, New York 10011

American Orthopsychiatric
Association, Inc.
1775 Broadway
New York, New York 10019

American Psychological Association
1200 17th Street N.W.
Washington, D.C. 20036

Association for the Care of
Children's Health
3615 Wisconsin Avenue N.W.
Washington, D.C. 20016

Association for Childhood Education
International
11141 Georgia Avenue
Suite 200
Wheaton, Maryland 20902

Association for Supervision and
Curriculum Development
1701 K Street N.W.
Washington, D.C. 20006

Association of Teacher Educators
1900 Association Drive
Reston, Virginia 22091

BANANAS
Child Care Information, Referral,
and Support Service
6501 Telegraph Avenue
Oakland, California 94609

BASICS
P.O. Box 604
Park Forest, Illinois 60466

California Child Care Resource and
Referral Network
320 Judah Street
Suite 2
San Francisco, California 94122

Center for Parenting Studies
Wheelock College
200 The Riverway
Boston, Massachusetts 12215

Child Care Action Campaign
99 Hudson Street
Room 1233
New York, New York 10013

Child Care Information Center
532 Settlers Landing Road
P.O. Box 548
Hampton, Virginia 23669

Child Care Information Exchange
P.O. Box 2890
Redmond, Washington 98073

Child Care Law Center
625 Market Street
Suite 815
San Francisco, California 94105

Child Care Resource Center
552 Massachusetts Avenue
Cambridge, Massachusetts 02139

Child Care Support Center
Save the Children South States
Office
1182 West Peachtree Street N.W.
Suite 209
Atlanta, Georgia 30303

Children's Defense Fund
122 C. Street N.W.
Washington, D.C. 20001

Children's Foundation
1420 New York Avenue N.W.
Suite 800
Washington, D.C. 20005

Child Study Association of America
9 East 89th Street
New York, New York 10003

Child Welfare League of America
67 Irving Place
New York, New York 10003

Council for Early Childhood
Professional Recognition
CDA National Credentialing
Program
1718 Connecticut Avenue N.W.
Washington, D.C. 20009

Council for Educational Development and Research
1518 K Street N.W.
#206
Washington, D.C. 20005

Council for Exceptional Children
1920 Association Drive
Reston, Virginia 22091

Council on Interracial Books for Children
Racism/Sexism Resource Center
1841 Broadway
New York, New York 10023

Day Care Council of New York
22 West 38th Street
New York, New York 10018

Early Childhood Education Council of New York City
66 Leroy Street
New York, New York 10014

Education Commission of the States
1860 Lincoln Avenue
Denver, Colorado 80295

Education Development Center
55 Chapel Street
Newton, Massachusetts 02160

ERIC/Clearinghouse on Elementary and Early Childhood Education
University of Illinois
College of Education
805 W. Penn Avenue
Urbana, Illinois 61801

Family Resource Coalition
230 North Michigan Avenue
Suite 1625
Chicago, Illinois 60601

Family Service Association of America
44 E. 23rd Street
New York, New York 10010

Gesell Institute for Human Development
310 Prospect Street
New Haven, Connecticut 06501

High/Scope Educational Research Foundation
600 N. River Street
Ypsilanti, Michigan 48197

International Montessori Society
912 Thayer Avenue
Columbus, Ohio 43215

Military Early Childhood Alliance
934 Avenida del Sol N.E.
Albuquerque, New Mexico 87110

National Association for Child Care Management
1800 M Street N.W.
Suite 1030 N
Washington, D.C. 20036

National Association for the Education of Young Children
1834 Connecticut Avenue N.W.
Washington, D.C. 20009

National Association for Family Day Care
P.O. Box 5778
Nashville, Tennessee 37208

National Association of Administrators of State and Federal Education Programs
1902 Lundwood Avenue
Ann Arbor, Michigan 40103

National Association of Early Childhood Specialists in State Department of Education
P.O. Box 2019
Trenton, New Jersey 08625

National Association of Hospital
Affiliated Child Care Programs
c/o Rush-Presbyterian St. Luke's
Medical Center
Lawrence Aronour Day School
630 S. Ashland
Chicago, Illinois 60607

National Association of State Boards
of Education
444 N. Capital Street N.W.
Washington, D.C. 20001

National Black Child Development
Institute
1463 Rhode Island Avenue N.W.
Washington, D.C. 20005

National Center for Clinical Infant
Programs
733 15th Street N.W.
Suite 912
Washington, D.C. 20005

National Center for Health
Education
30 E. 29th Street
New York, New York 10016

National Certificate for Child Care
Professionals
5701 Beechnut
Houston, Texas 77074

National Committee for the
Prevention of Child Abuse
Suite 510
111 E. Wacker Drive
Chicago, Illinois 60601

National Congress of Parents and
Teachers
1201 16th Street N.W.
Washington, D.C. 20036

National Council of Churches
Child Day Care Project

National Council of Churches in
the U.S.A.
Child Advocacy Office
475 Riverside Drive
Room 572
New York, New York 10025

National Education Association
1201 16th Street N.W.
Washington, D.C. 20036

National Employer-Supported
Child Care Project
P.O. Box 40652
Pasadena, California 91104

National Family Day Care Providers
Network
5730 Market Street
Oakland, California 94608

National Independent Private
Schools Associations
2355 Lake Street
San Francisco, California 94121

National Institute of Child Health
and Human Development
National Institute of Health
Building 31
Room 2A34
Bethesda, Maryland 20014

National Kindergarten Association
8 West 40th Street
New York, New York 10018

Non-Sexist Child Development
Project
Women's Action Alliance Inc.
370 Lexington Avenue
Room 603
New York, New York 10017

Parent Cooperative Preschools
International
P.O. Box 31335
Phoenix, Arizona 85046

Professional Association for Childhood Education
352 Harper Lane
Danville, California 94526

Resources for Child Care Management
P.O. Box 669
Summit, New Jersey 07901

Resources for Child Caring Inc.
906 N. Dale Street
St. Paul, Minnesota 55103

Resources for Infant Education
1550 Murray Circle
Los Angeles, California 90026

School-Age Child Care Project
Wellesley College
Center for Research on Women
Wellesley, Massachusetts 02181

Society for Research in Child Development
University of Chicago Press
5801 Ellis Avenue
Chicago, Illinois 60637

Southern Association for Children Under Six
Box 5403
Brady Station
Little Rock, Arkansas 72215

State Higher Education Executive Officers
One American Place
Suite 1530
Baton Rouge, Louisiana 70825

USA Toy Library Association
5940 W. Touhy Avenue
Chicago, Illinois 60648

SOURCES OF EQUIPMENT/MATERIALS FOR EARLY CHILDHOOD EDUCATION

ABC School Supply, Inc.
437 Armour Circle N.E.
P.O. Box 13086
Atlanta, Georgia 30324

Angeles Toys, Inc.
8106 Allport Avenue
Santa Fe Springs, California 90670

The Barrington Company
P.O. Box 513
Barrington, Illinois 60010

Big Toys
2601 South Hood Street
Tacoma, Washington 98409

Center for Applied Research in Education
Route 59 at Brookhill Drive
West Nyack, New York 10995–9901

Child Care Concepts
P.O. 1341
Department D 3
Orem, Utah 84057

Childcraft Educational Corporation
20 Kilmer Road
Edison, New Jersey 08818

Children's Learning Center, Inc.
6113 Allisonville Road
Indianapolis, Indiana 46220

Children's Playgrounds Inc.
2014 Massachusetts Avenue
Cambridge, Massachusetts 02238

Children's Press
1224 West Van Buren Street
Chicago, Illinois 60607

Climbing Things
P.O. Box 1283
Tampa, Florida 33601

Community Playthings
Route 213
Rifton, New York 12471

Constructive Playthings
2008 W. 103rd Terrace
Leawood, Kansas 66206

Creative Curriculum, Inc.
15681 Commerce Lane
Huntingdon Beach, California 92649

Creative Playthings
P.O. Box 1100
Princeton, New Jersey 08540

Dandi-Lion
8920 S.W. Edgewood Street
Rigard, Oregon 97223

Dinosaurs 'n Donuts
P.O. Box 99132 E
Tacoma, Washington 98499–0132

Curriculum Associates
6 Henshaw Street
Woburn, Massachusetts 01801

Delta Education Inc.
P.O. Box M
Nashua, New Hampshire 03061

T.S. Dennison and Company
Suite M 705
9601 Newton Avenue South
Minneapolis, Minnesota 55431

Didax Educational Resources
6 Doulton Place
Peabody, Massachusetts 01960

Early Childhood Book House
822 N.W. 23rd
Portland, Oregon 97210

EBSCO Curriculum Materials
Box 486
Birmingham, Alabama 35201

Economy Company
P.O. Box 25308
1901 N. Walnut Street
Oklahoma City, Oklahoma 73125

EDUCAT Publishers Inc.
P.O. Box 2891
Clinton, Iowa 52735

Educational Activities Inc.
P.O. Box 87
Baldwin, New York 11510

Educational Aids
845 Wisteria Drive
Fremont, California 94538

Educational Teaching Aids
159 W. Kinzie Street
Chicago, Illinois 60610

Greenwillow Books
Box CM-EDEC
105 Madison Avenue
New York, New York 10016

Growing Child
P.O. Box 620
Lafayette, Indiana 47902

Grune and Stratton Inc.
111 Fifth Avenue
New York, New York 10003

Gryphon House Inc.
P.O. Box 275
Mt. Ranier, Maryland 20712

Hammett Company
Early Childhood Division
Box 545
Braintree, Massachusetts 02184

High/Scope Foundation
600 N. River Street
Ypsilanti, Michigan 48197

Hospital Play Equipment Company
1122 Judson Avenue
Evanston, Illinois 60602

Human Sciences Press Inc.
72 Fifth Avenue
New York, New York 10011

Humnics Ltd.
P.O. Box 7447
Atlanta, Georgia 30309

Ideal School Supply Company
11000 S. Labergne Avenue
Oakland, Illinois 60453

Instructo/McGraw-Hill
Malvern, Pennsylvania 19355

Instructors Preschool Book Club
Department W
40 Guernsey Street
P.O. Box 10339
Stamford, Connecticut 06904–9928

It's Child's Play Curriculum, Inc.
5829 N.W. 86th
Oklahoma City, Oklahoma 73132

Johnson and Johnson Baby Products Division
Child Development Products
Grandview Road
Skillman, New Jersey 08558

Kaplan Corporation
600 Jonestown Road
Winston-Salem, North Carolina 27103

Knowledge Tree Group
360 Park Avenue South
New York, New York 10010

Lakeshore Curriculum Materials Company
16463 Phoebe Avenue
La Mirada, California 90637

Landscape Structures, Inc.
601 7th Street South
Delano, Minnesota 55328

Learning Line
P.O. Box 1200
Palo Alto, California 94302

Lego Systems Inc.
555 Raylor Road
Enfield, Connecticut 06082

Lexington Books
125 Spring Street
Lexington, Massachusetts 02173

Little Peoples Workshop
Box 99608
Louisville, Kentucky 40299

London Bridge
P.O. Box 5964
1205 Greenwood Road
Baltimore, Maryland 21208

Milton Bradley Company
Springfield, Massachusetts 01101

National Dairy Council
6300 N. River Road
Rosemont, Illinois 60018

Nienhous Montessori USA, Inc.
320 Pioneer Way
Department 4
Mountain View, California 94041

NOVO Educational Toy and Equipment Corporation
124 W. 24th Street
New York, New York 10011

Parent Cooperative Preschools International
P.O. Box 31335
Phoenix, Arizona 85046

Parenting Press
7750 31st Avenue N.E.
Seattle, Washington 98115

Parker Publishing Company
Route 59 at Brookhill Drive
West Nyack, NY 10995–9901

Pitman Learning Inc.
6 Davis Drive
Belmont, California 94002

Playhouse
1406 32nd Avenue
San Francisco, California 94122

Preschool Curriculum Resources
P.O. Box 319
Redding Ridge, Connecticut 06876

Princeton Center for Infancy
306 Alexander Street
Princeton, New Jersey 08450

Professional Association for Childhood Education
352 Harper Lane
Danville, California 94526

Programs for Education Inc.
Box 858
Lumberville, Pennsylvania 18933

Puppet Productions Inc.
P.O. Box 82008
San Diego, California 92138

Quisenaire Company of America, Inc.
12 Church Street
New Rochelle, New York 10805

R and E Research Associates Inc.
936 Industrial Avenue
Palo Alto, California 94303

Resources for Child Care Management
P.O. Box 669
Summit, New Jersey 07901

Resources for Child Caring Inc.
906 N. Dale Street
St. Paul, Minnesota 55103

Resources for Children in Hospitals
P.O. Box 10
Belmont, Massachusetts 02178

Resources for Infant Education
1550 Murray Circle
Los Angeles, California 90026

Rhythm Band Inc.
P.O. Box 126
Ft. Worth, Texas 76101

Salco Toys Inc.
Route 1
Nerstand, Minnesota 55053

Schocken Books
200 Madison Avenue
New York, New York 10016

Scholastic Book Services
904 Sylvan Avenue
Englewood Cliffs, New Jersey 07632

School-Age Child Care Project
Wellesley College
Center for Research on Women
Wellesley, Massachusetts 02181

School-Age Notes
P.O. Box 120674
Nashville, Tennessee 73212

Schoolyard Big Toys
Northwest Design Products
3113 S. Pine Street
Tacoma, Washington 98409

Science Research Associates Inc.
259 E. Erie Street
Chicago, Illinois 60611

Scott, Foresman Company
1900 E. Lake Avenue
Glenview, Illinois 60025

Silver Burdett Company
250 James Street
Morristown, New Jersey 07960

Society for Research in Child Development
University of Chicago Press
5801 Ellis Avenue
Chicago, Illinois 60637

Southern Association for Children Under Six
Box 5403
Brady Station
Little Rock, Arkansas 72215

State Higher Education Executive Officers
One American Place
Suite 1530
Baton Rouge, Louisiana 70825

Snow Corporation
P.O. Box 9800
Ft. Worth, Texas 97107

Special Learning Corporation
P.O. Box 306
Cuilford, Connecticut 06437

Spectrum Educational Supplies Inc.
P.O. Box 6607
Bridgewater, New Jersey 08807

Stone Canyon Press
P.O. Box 12866
Dallas, Texas 75225

Swallow Inc.
2412 Kensington Drive
Columbus, Ohio 43221

Teachers College Press
Teachers College
Columbia University
New York, New York 10027

Teaching Resources Corporation
50 Pond Park Road
Hingham, Massachusetts 02043

Toys 'n Things
Training and Resource Center Inc.
906 N. Sale Street
Box 19
St. Paul, Minnesota 55103

Toys to Grow On
P.O. Box 17
Long Beach, California 90801

Trend Enterprises
Box 3073
St. Paul, Minnesota 55165

Troubador Press
385 Fremont Street
San Francisco, California 94105

Tyco Toys Inc.
6000 Midlantic Drive
Mt. Laurel, New Jersey 08054

USA Toy Library Association
5940 W. Touhy Avenue
Chicago, Illinois 60648

VORT Corporation
P.O. Box 11757A
Palo Alto, California 94306

Wingbow Press
2940 7th Street
Box D
Berkley, California 94710

Wood Etc. Corporation
940 N. Beltine
#137
P.O. Box 3484E
Irving, Texas 75061

Woodland Structures Inc.
3539 85th Avenue North
Brooklyn, Minnesota 55443

Yale University Press
92 A Yale Station
New Haven, Connecticut 06520

DEPARTMENTS OF EDUCATION*

Superintendent of Education
State Department of Education
501 Dexter Avenue
481 State Office Building
Montgomery, Alabama 36130

Commissioner of Education
State Department of Education
State Office Building, Pouch F
Juneau, Alaska 99811

Superintendent of Public Instruction
State Department of Education
1535 West Jefferson
Phoenix, Arizona 85007

Director, General Education Div.
Department of Education
#4 Capital Mall
Little Rock, Arkansas 72201–1071

Superintendent of Public Instruction
State Department of Education
721 Capital Mall
Sacramento, California 94222–2720

Commissioner of Education
State Department of Education
201 East Colfax Avenue Goldbelt
Denver, Colorado 80203–1705

Commissioner of Education
State Department of Education
165 Capital Avenue
Room 308, State Office Building
Hartford, Connecticut 06106

Superintendent of Education
Commonwealth of the Northern
Mariana Islands
Department of Education
Saipan, Northern Mariana Islands
96950

Executive Director
Council of Chief State School
Officers
379 Hall of the States
400 North Capital Street N.W.
Washington, D.C. 20001

Superintendent of Public Schools
District of Columbia Public Schools
415 12th Street N.W.
Washington, D.C. 20004

Superintendent of Public Instruction
State Department of Instruction
P.O. Box 1402
Townsend Building, #279
Federal and Lockerman Streets
Dover, Delaware 19903

Commissioner of Education
State Department of Education
Capital Building, Room PL 116
Tallahassee, Florida 32399

Superintendent of Schools
State Department of Education
Twin Towers East
Capital Square
Atlanta, Georgia 30334–5020

Director of Education
Department of Education
P.O. Box DE
Agana, Guam 96910

Superintendent of Education
Department of Education
P.O. Box 2360
#307
1390 Miller Street
Honolulu, Hawaii 96804

* "Directory of Chief State School Officers," (Washington, DC: Council of Chief State School Officers, August 1988).

Superintendent of Public Instruction
State Department of Education
650 West State Street
Boise, Idaho 83720

Superintendent of Education
State Department of Education
100 North First Street
Springfield, Illinois 62777

Superintendent of Public Instruction
State Department of Education
#229
100 North Capital Street
Indianapolis, Indiana 46204–2798

Director of Education
State Department of Education
Grimes State Office Building
East 14th and Grand Streets
Des Moines, Iowa 50319–0146

Commissioner of Education
State Department of Education
120 East 10th Street
Topeka, Kansas 66612

Superintendent of Public Instruction
State Department of Education
1725 Capital Plaza Tower
Frankfort, Kentucky 40601

Superintendent of Education
State Department of Education
Post Office Box 94064
626 North 4th Street
Baton Rouge, Louisiana 70804–9064

Commissioner of Education
Department of Educational and
Cultural Services
State House, Station #23
Augusta, Maine 04333

State Superintendent of Schools
State Department of Education
200 West Baltimore Street
Baltimore, Maryland 21201

Commissioner of Education
State Department of Education
Quincy Center Plaza
1385 Hancock Street
Quincy, Massachusetts 02169

Superintendent of Public Instruction
State Department of Education
P.O. Box 30008
115 West Allegan Street
Lansing, Michigan 48909

Commissioner of Education
State Department of Education
712 Capital Square Building
550 Cedar Street
St. Paul, Minnesota 55101

Superintendent of Education
State Department of Education
P.O. Box 771
High Street
Jackson, Mississippi 39205–0771

Commissioner of Education
Department of Elementary and
Secondary Education
P.O. Box 480
6th Floor
205 Jefferson Street
Jefferson City, Missouri 65102

Superintendent of Public Instruction
State Department of Education
106 State Capital
Helena, Montana 59620

Commissioner of Education
State Department of Education
Post Office Box 94987
301 Centennial Mall South
Lincoln, Nebraska 68509

Superintendent of Public Instruction
State Department of Education
400 West King Street
Capital Complex
Carson City, Nevada 89710

Commissioner of Education
State Department of Education
101 Pleasant Street
State Office Park South
Concord, New Hampshire 03301

Commissioner of Education
State Department of Education
225 West State Street
Trenton, New Jersey 08625

Superintendent of Public Instruction
State Department of Education
Building
300 Don Gaspar
Santa Fe, New Mexico 87501–2786

Commissioner of Education
State Department of Education
111 Education Building
Washington Ave.
Albany, New York 12234

Superintendent of Public Instruction
State Dept. of Public Instruction
Education Building, Room 318
Edenton and Salisbury Streets
Raleigh, North Carolina 27603–1712

Superintendent of Public Instruction
State Department of Public
Instruction
State Capital Building, 11th Floor
600 Boulevard Avenue East
Bismarck, Nor+h Dakota
58505–0164

Superintendent of Public Instruction
State Department of Education
Room 808
65 South Front Street
Columbus, Ohio 43266–0308

Superintendent of Public Instruction
State Department of Education
Oliver Hodge Memorial Education
Building
2500 North Lincoln Blvd.
Oklahoma City, Oklahoma
73105–4599

Superintendent of Public Instruction
State Department of Education
700 Pringle Parkway S.E.
Salem, Oregon, 97310

Secretary of Education
State Department of Education
10th Floor
333 Market Street
Harrisburg, Pennsylvania 17126

Secretary of Education
Department of Education
Post Office Box 759
Hato Rey, Puerto Rico 00919

Commissioner of Education
State Department of Education
22 Hayes Street
Providence, Rhode Island 02908

Superintendent of Education
State Department of Education
1006 Rutledge Building
1429 Senate Street
Columbia, South Carolina 29201

State Superintendent
State Department of Education
Division of Education
700 Governors Drive
Pierre, South Dakota 57501

Commissioner of Education
State Department of Education
100 Cordell Hull Building
Nashville, Tennessee 37219

Commissioner of Education
Texas Education Agency
William B. Travis Building
1701 N. Congress Avenue
Austin, Texas 78701

Director of Education
Department of Education
Pago Pago, Tutuila 96799

Superintendent of Public Instruction
State Office of Education
250 East 500 South
Salt Lake City, Utah 84111

Commissioner of Education
State Department of Education
120 State Street
Montpelier, Vermont 05602–2703

Superintendent of Public Instruction
State Department of Education
Post Office Box 6Q
James Monroe Building
Fourteenth and Franklin Streets
Richmond, Virginia 23216–2060

Commissioner of Education
Department of Education
44–46 Kongens Gade
St. Thomas, Virgin Islands 00802

Superintendent of Public Instruction
State Department of Public Instruction
Old Capital Building
Washington and Legion
Mail Stop FG-11
Olympia, Washington 98504

State Superintendent of Schools
State Department of Education
1900 Washington Street
Building B, Room 385
Charleston, West Virginia 25305

Superintendent of Public Instruction
State Department of Education
125 South Webster Street
P.O. Box 7841
Madison, Wisconsin 53707

Superintendent of Public Instruction
State Department of Education
Hathaway Building
Cheyenne, Wyoming 82002